THE
MUFFIN BIBLE

THE
MUFFIN BIBLE
HEAVENLY MUFFIN RECIPES

PENGUIN BOOKS

PENGUIN BOOKS

Penguin Books (NZ) Ltd, cnr Airborne and Rosedale Roads, Albany, Auckland 1310, New Zealand
Penguin Books Ltd, 27 Wrights Lane, London W8 5TZ, England
Penguin Putnam Inc, 375 Hudson Street, New York, NY 10014, United States
Penguin Books Australia Ltd, 487 Maroondah Highway, Ringwood, Australia 3134
Penguin Books Canada Ltd, 10 Alcorn Avenue, Toronto, Ontario, Canada M4V 3B2
Penguin Books (South Africa) Pty Ltd, 5 Watkins Street, Denver Ext 4, 2094, South Africa
Penguin Books India (P) Ltd, 11, Community Centre, Panchsheel Park, New Delhi 110 017, India
Penguin Books Ltd, Registered Offices: Harmondsworth, Middlesex, England

First published by Penguin Books (NZ) Ltd, 2001

3 5 7 9 10 8 6 4 2

Copyright © this selection, Penguin Books (NZ) Ltd, 2001

Designed and typeset by Neo Publishing
Printed in Australia by McPherson's Printing Group

ISBN 0 14 301800 0
www.penguin.co.nz

Hints for Making the Best Muffins

There are many useful tips for improving the taste and texture of your muffins, but they will all be to no avail if you overmix your batter – tough muffins can be a tough lesson. You should mix just enough to combine the wet and dry ingredients.

Preheat the oven to the required temperature and grease the muffin pans before you start. Also, have a read through the recipe before you begin so that you have all the chopping, grating and blending done before you start mixing the ingredients. The less time spent mixing things together, the better. Too much liquid in the mixture will result in soggy and flat muffins. Too little liquid and they'll end up hard and dry. Also, white flour instead of wholemeal will give you a lighter muffin.

Bake the muffins in the middle of the oven, and be adaptable with the temperature and timing of cooking – every oven behaves differently. The oven is too hot if the muffin tops are uneven and cracked, and it is too cool if the tops are pale and have not risen.

If microwaving bran muffins, mix oil and bran first, then mix it with the rest of the ingredients. This will result in a more moist muffin. When you take the muffins out of the oven, leave them to stand for two or three minutes.

To re-heat muffins, wrap them loosely in aluminium foil and put in the oven for five to ten minutes at 125°C, or 15 to 20 minutes at 180°C if they are frozen.

Almond Chip Muffins

1 3/4 cups self-raising flour
2–3 tblsp caster sugar
1 tsp baking powder
1/2 tsp salt
1 egg
3/4 cup milk
1/3 cup butter, melted
2 tsp grated lemon peel
1/2 tsp vanilla essence
3/4 cup chopped, unblanched almonds

IN large bowl, sift together flour, sugar, baking powder and salt. In small bowl, combine egg, milk, melted butter, grated lemon peel, vanilla and almonds. Add to flour mixture. With a fork, stir briskly until all dry ingredients are moistened. Batter should look lumpy. Three-quarters fill greased muffin pans and bake at 200°C for 20–25 minutes or until golden brown.

Almond Poppy Seed Muffins

1 egg
³/₄ tsp salt
¹/₃ cup sugar
¹/₄ cup oil
1 cup milk
2 cups flour
1 tblsp baking powder
³/₄ cup chopped almonds
¹/₃ cup poppy seeds

PREHEAT oven to 200°C. Beat egg, salt and sugar until light and fluffy. Add oil in a stream and continue beating. Beat in milk. Sift flour and baking powder together several times and add to batter, stirring until just mixed. Add nuts and poppy seeds. Bake in greased muffin pans for 20–25 minutes.

American Muffins

1 cup flour
1 tblsp baking powder
$^1/_3$ cup sugar
1 egg
$^1/_3$ cup milk
75g butter, softened
75g frozen blackberries or blackcurrants, partly thawed
2 tblsp sugar for sprinkling
1 tsp ground cinnamon for sprinkling

IN large bowl mix together flour, baking powder and sugar. In separate bowl whisk egg and milk together and beat in butter. Mix liquid ingredients into dry ingredients and stir until combined. Fold in berries gently. Spoon batter into muffin pans and sprinkle over a little sugar and cinnamon mixed together. Bake at 180°C for 20 minutes.

Anzac Muffins

1 tsp baking soda
3/4 cup warm milk
50g butter, melted
2 tblsp golden syrup
2/3 cup brown sugar
1/2 cup desiccated coconut
1 tsp baking powder
1/2 cup rolled oats
1 egg
2 cups flour

DISSOLVE baking soda in milk, then add butter, golden syrup and brown sugar and mix well. Add remaining ingredients and stir until just combined. Three-quarters fill well-greased muffin pans and bake at 190°C for 15–20 minutes.

Apple Muffins

$^1/_3$ cup vegetable oil
$^3/_4$ cup firmly packed brown sugar
1 tblsp liquid honey
2 eggs, lightly beaten
1 cup grated apple
$^1/_2$ cup apple juice
1 $^1/_2$ cups All-bran
1 cup wholemeal flour
$^1/_2$ cup plain flour
1 $^1/_2$ tsp baking powder
$^1/_2$ cup buttermilk

MIX oil, brown sugar and honey. Add lightly beaten eggs and beat until thoroughly combined. Add grated apple and apple juice. Stir in All-bran. Sift dry ingredients. Stir into egg mixture with buttermilk until just combined. Three-quarters fill greased muffin pans and bake at 220°C for 15 minutes or until firm.

Apple Muffins with Maple Glaze

1 ¹/₃ cups flour
1 cup oats – quick or old-fashioned
¹/₂ cup sugar
1 tblsp baking powder
2 tsp ground cinnamon
¹/₂ cup milk
¹/₃ cup butter, melted
¹/₄ cup maple syrup
2 egg whites, lightly beaten
1 cup chopped apple
toasted pecan halves
Glaze
¹/₄ cup icing sugar
1 ¹/₂ tblsp maple syrup

PREHEAT oven to 200°C. Mix flour, oats, sugar, baking powder and cinnamon. Mix milk, butter, syrup and egg whites. Mix wet and dry ingredients until just blended. Gently stir in apple. Three-quarters fill muffin pans. Top each with a pecan half. Bake 20–25 minutes. Let stand a few minutes then remove from pans. Cool about 10 minutes. **Glaze**: Mix together icing sugar and maple syrup. Leave muffins sitting on cooling rack under which you have placed sheets of waxed paper. Drizzle over glaze.

Apple, Carrot & Raisin Muffins

2 cups flour
4 tsp baking powder
$^1/_2$ tsp salt
4 tblsp brown sugar
1 tsp mixed spice
1 tsp cinnamon
1 cup bran
2 apples, peeled, cored and grated
1 cup grated carrot
$^1/_2$ cup raisins
2 eggs
$^1/_4$–$^1/_2$ cup milk
$^1/_2$ cup oil

SIFT flour, baking powder, salt, sugar, mixed spice and cinnamon together. Add bran, apple, carrot and raisins and mix well. Make a well in centre. Lightly beat eggs and milk and pour into well. Add oil. Mix thoroughly. Spoon into greased muffin pans and bake at 220°C for 15–20 minutes.

Apple, Date & Bran Muffins

2 eggs
$1/2$ cup brown sugar
$1/4$ cup oil
2 cups Trim milk
1 cup chopped dates
1 cup raisins
1 cup grated green apple
$1/2$ tsp cinnamon
1 cup bran
2 cups flour
$1/2$ cup wheatgerm
2 tsp baking soda
2 tsp baking powder

BEAT eggs lightly. Add sugar, oil, milk, dates and raisins, and stir to mix. Combine rest of ingredients and stir in egg mixture. Cover and chill for at least one hour. Three-quarters fill greased muffin pans and bake at 190°C for 20 minutes or until firm.

Apple-Nut Muffins

1 egg
$^2/_3$ cup apple juice or milk
$^1/_2$ cup oil
1 tsp vanilla essence
2 cups flour
$^1/_4$ cup sugar
$^1/_4$ cup brown sugar, packed
1 tblsp baking powder
$^1/_2$ tsp salt
$^1/_2$ cup chopped nuts
1 chopped apple
cinnamon sugar

IN bowl, beat egg with juice, oil and vanilla. Stir in flour, sugars, baking powder and salt until just moistened. Stir in nuts and apple. Three-quarters fill prepared muffin pans (greased or paper-lined). Sprinkle with cinnamon sugar (1 tsp cinnamon and 2 tblsp sugar mixed together). Bake at 200°C for 20 minutes or until golden brown.

Apple & Tamarillo Muffins

1 egg
³/₄ cup milk
100g butter, melted
2 cups flour
1 tblsp baking powder
¹/₂ cup sugar
1 cup grated apple
3 tamarillos, peeled and chopped

MIX all ingredients until just combined. Grease muffin pans and three-quarters fill with mixture. Bake at 180°C for 15 minutes.

Apricot & Almond Muffins

1 cup dried apricots
2 cups flour
1 egg
³/₄ cup milk
75g butter, melted
1 tblsp baking powder
¹/₂ cup sugar
70g almond slivers

COVER apricots with water and bring to the boil. Leave to cool for at least one hour then drain, chop and transfer to a bowl. Add remaining ingredients and mix until just combined. Spoon into well-greased muffin pans and bake at 180°C for 15 minutes.

Apricot & Lemon Muffins

1 cup flour
$1/2$ tsp salt
1 tsp baking powder
1 $1/2$ cups bran
$1/4$ cup sugar
$1/2$ cup chopped apricots, dried or fresh
2 tsp grated lemon rind
$1/2$ tsp baking soda
1 cup milk
1 egg
1 tblsp butter, melted
1 tblsp golden syrup

SIFT flour, salt and baking powder. Stir in bran, sugar, chopped apricots and grated lemon rind. Make a well in centre of dry ingredients. Dissolve baking soda in milk. Beat egg lightly. Combine milk, melted butter, egg and golden syrup, and pour onto dry ingredients. Stir to just combine. Three-quarters fill greased muffin pans and bake at 200°C for 10–15 minutes or until firm.

Apricot & Walnut Muffins

12 dried apricots
2 tblsp brandy
2 cups flour
1 tblsp baking powder
$^1/_2$ cup sugar
$^1/_2$ cup chopped walnuts
1 egg
$^1/_2$ cup milk
50g butter, melted

COOK apricots in brandy for five minutes and then roughly chop. Sift flour and baking powder and stir in sugar, chopped apricots and chopped walnuts. Combine egg and milk and add melted butter. Make a well in centre of dry ingredients and pour in milk and butter. Stir quickly until just combined. Three-quarters fill greased muffin pans and bake at 200°C for 15–20 minutes.

Arkansas Oatmeal 'n' Brown Sugar Muffins

1 cup wholemeal flour
1 cup raw wheatgerm
1 tblsp baking powder
$^1/_2$ tsp salt
$^1/_3$ tsp brown sugar, firmly packed
3 tblsp butter
1 large egg
1 cup oatmeal, cooked and cooled
1 $^1/_3$ cups milk
$^1/_2$ cup raisins (optional)

MIX flour, wheatgerm, baking powder, salt and sugar in large bowl. Cut in butter using fingertips. Using wooden spoon or wire whisk, beat egg, oatmeal and milk in second bowl to blend well. Stir oatmeal mixture into flour mixture until just combined. Quickly fold in raisins. Spoon batter into prepared muffin pans, filling each three-quarters full. Bake at 215°C for 18–20 minutes.

Artichoke Heart with Bacon & Garlic Muffins

³/₄ cup fresh breadcrumbs
1 clove crushed garlic
2 tblsp butter
1 egg, beaten
¹/₂ cup flour
¹/₄ tsp salt
1 tblsp baking powder
¹/₂ cup grated cheese
1 cup artichoke hearts, quartered
2 rashers bacon, cooked and chopped

FRY breadcrumbs and garlic in butter until crisp. Make egg up to 1 cup with water and mix with flour, salt, baking powder, cheese, artichokes and bacon until just combined. Three-quarters fill well-greased muffin pans and sprinkle with fried breadcrumbs. Bake at 200°C for 12–15 minutes.

Bacon & Cheese Muffins

1 cup flour
¹/₂ tsp salt
1 tsp baking powder
1 ¹/₂ cups bran
¹/₄ cup sugar
¹/₂ tsp baking soda
1 ¹/₂ cups milk
1 egg
1 tblsp butter, melted
1 tblsp golden syrup
3 rashers cooked bacon
1 cup grated tasty cheese

SIFT flour, salt and baking powder. Stir in bran and sugar, and make a well in the centre. Dissolve baking soda in milk. Beat egg lightly. Combine milk, melted butter, egg and golden syrup. Add chopped bacon and cheese to dry ingredients, then pour in milk mixture. Stir until just combined. Three-quarters fill greased muffin pans and bake at 200°C for 10–15 minutes.

Bacon & Egg Filo Muffins

6 sheets filo pastry
melted butter
7 eggs
$^1/_4$ cup water
$^1/_4$ cup milk
$^1/_2$ tsp salt
3 rashers bacon, cooked and chopped
1 tblsp parsley, chopped

BRUSH filo pastry sheets with butter, stack and cut into six squares. Line well-greased muffin pans with pastry squares. Beat one egg with water, milk, salt, bacon and parsley, then divide evenly among the 'muffins'. Break an egg into each muffin. Bake at 190°C for approximately 15–20 minutes, until egg is set. Serve hot.

Bacon & Tomato Muffins

2 cups flour
1 tblsp baking powder
4 rashers bacon
2 tomatoes
2 tblsp tomato paste
1 egg
³/₄ cup milk
50g butter, melted

SIFT flour and baking powder. Cut rind off bacon and chop flesh. Skin and de-seed tomatoes, and chop roughly. Mix bacon, tomatoes, tomato paste, egg and milk together. Pour tomato mixture and melted butter into dry ingredients. Stir until just combined. Three-quarters fill greased muffin pans and bake at 200°C for 15–20 minutes.

Baileys, Cream Cheese & Chocolate Muffins

90g cream cheese
1 ½ tblsp Baileys Irish Cream
1 egg
¾ cup milk
⅓ cup water
50g butter, melted
100g chocolate, grated
1 ½ cups flour
2 tsp baking powder
½ tsp salt
3 tblsp cocoa
½ cup sugar

BEAT cream cheese until smooth, add Baileys and beat again. In separate bowl whisk egg, milk, water and butter, then add chocolate. Sift remaining dry ingredients into egg mixture and stir until just combined. One-third fill well-greased muffin pans with muffin mixture, make a hollow in centre, and fill with 1 teaspoon cream cheese mixture. Top up to three-quarters full with remaining muffin mixture. Bake at 190°C for 20 minutes.

Banana Choc Chip Muffins

1 1/2 cups self-raising flour
1/3 cup caster sugar
60g butter
2/3 cup mashed banana
1/2 cup chocolate chips
1 egg
1/2 cup milk
Filling
sliced banana
whipped cream

IN large bowl rub together flour, sugar and butter until mixture resembles fine breadcrumbs. Stir in mashed banana, chocolate chips, egg and milk to combine. Spoon mixture into prepared muffin pans and bake at 190°C for 20 minutes. Fold sliced banana into whipped cream and use to fill muffins.

Banana & Date Muffins

2 1/2 cups oat bran
1 1/2 cups wholemeal flour
6 tsp baking powder
2 tsp mixed spice
1 tsp cinnamon
500g finely chopped banana
100g finely chopped dates
1/2 cup apple juice concentrate
1/2 cup cold-pressed grapeseed oil
1 cup evaporated milk
3 egg whites

PLACE oat bran in a bowl. Add sifted wholemeal flour, baking powder, mixed spice and cinnamon. Distribute flour and spices through oat bran with hands. Add banana and dates and toss well to break up and coat with flour. Combine apple juice concentrate, oil and milk, and combine with flour and oat mixture. Beat egg whites until soft, and gently fold through the mixture. Three-quarters fill greased muffin pans and bake at 180°C for 25–30 minutes.

Banana & Ginger Muffins

60g butter
2 tblsp sugar
1 egg
1 ripe banana, mashed
1 cup flour
1 tsp ground ginger
2 tblsp golden syrup
1 tsp baking soda
$1/3$ cup milk
Filling
whipped cream
sugar
ground ginger

CREAM butter and sugar together, then add egg and mashed banana. Sift in flour and ginger. Dissolve syrup and baking soda in milk and add to mixture. Mix lightly. Spoon batter into prepared muffin pans and bake at 200°C for 15 minutes. Serve filled with fresh whipped cream flavoured with a little sugar and ground ginger.

Banana Lemon Muffins

110g unsalted butter
1 ¼ cups sugar
2 large eggs
1 cup mashed banana
2 tblsp lemon juice
1 tsp vanilla essence
2 cups flour
1 tsp baking soda
pinch of salt
¾ cup buttermilk (or use yoghurt or full cream milk)

GREASE muffin pans. Cream the butter and sugar until light and fluffy. Beat in eggs, one at a time. Whip in banana, lemon juice and vanilla. Sift flour, baking soda and salt together. Stir into banana mixture alternately with the buttermilk. Bake at 180°C for 20 minutes.

Banana Wholemeal Muffins

2 ripe bananas
1 egg
75g butter, melted
$^1/_2$ tsp baking soda
$^1/_2$ cup hot milk
1 $^1/_2$ cups wholemeal flour
2 tsp baking powder
$^1/_4$ tsp ground cinnamon
$^1/_4$ tsp ground nutmeg
$^1/_2$ cup brown sugar
$^1/_2$ cup sultanas

MASH bananas and add egg, butter and baking soda dissolved in milk. Add remaining ingredients and mix until just combined. Three-quarters fill well-greased muffin pans and bake at 200°C for 15–20 minutes.

Bean Sprout & Cottage Cheese Muffins

2 cups flour
4 tsp baking powder
$^1/_2$ tsp salt
$^1/_4$ tsp white pepper
1 tsp curry powder
1 $^1/_2$ cups unprocessed bran
100g butter
2 cups bean sprouts
1 egg
1 $^1/_4$ cups milk
1 cup cottage cheese with chives

S IFT flour, baking powder, salt, white pepper and curry powder. Stir in bran. Cut in butter until mixture resembles coarse breadcrumbs. Add bean sprouts. Make a well in centre of dry ingredients. Lightly beat egg and milk together. Add to dry ingredients. Stir until just combined. Fold in cottage cheese. Three-quarters fill greased muffin pans and bake at 200°C for 15–20 minutes.

Bennington Blueberry Maple Muffins

1 cup bran flakes, lightly crushed
1 cup sour cream
1 cup maple syrup
2 eggs
2 cups flour
2 tsp baking soda
1 cup blueberries
1 cup walnuts, chopped

THE night before baking, combine bran flakes with sour cream and maple syrup; refrigerate overnight. Grease muffin pans or line with paper cases. Beat eggs until frothy and blend into bran flake mixture. Combine flour with baking soda and stir into batter until blended. Fold in blueberries. Spoon batter into prepared pans; sprinkle walnuts evenly over muffins. Bake at 200°C for 15–20 minutes.

Best Blueberry Muffins

2 cups flour
1 tblsp baking powder
2 tsp custard powder
1 cup sugar
³/₄ cup blueberries (or blackcurrants)
2 eggs
³/₄ cup milk
³/₄ cup oil
icing sugar for dusting

S IFT flour, baking powder and custard powder into a bowl. Add sugar and blueberries. In separate bowl mix together eggs, milk and oil. Add milk mixture to dry ingredients and combine. Spoon batter into prepared muffin pans and bake at 190°C for 15–20 minutes. Serve dusted with icing sugar.

Black Bottom Muffins

1 1/4 cups flour
3/4 cup sugar
1/3 cup cocoa
1/2 tsp baking soda
1/4 tsp salt
2/3 cup buttermilk
1/4 cup oil
60g butter, melted and cooled slightly
1 egg
1 tsp vanilla essence
1/3 cup chocolate chips
Topping: 200g cream cheese, 1/4 cup sugar, 1 egg, 1/8 tsp almond essence,
1/4 cup toasted slivered almonds

IN large bowl mix together flour, sugar, cocoa, baking soda and salt. In separate bowl mix together buttermilk, oil, butter, egg and vanilla until well combined. Make a well in centre of dry ingredients and add buttermilk mixture. Stir to combine, then mix in chocolate chips. Spoon batter into prepared muffin pans, then cover with topping. Bake at 190°C for 20 minutes. To make topping, combine cream cheese, sugar, egg and almond essence, then fold in almonds.

Black Forest Muffins

1 egg
150g dark chocolate melted in 1 cup boiling water
75g butter, softened
2 cups flour
2 tsp baking powder
1 tblsp cocoa
1/2 cup caster sugar
1 cup glacé cherries
Filling
100g chocolate, melted
100g sour cream
1 1/2 cups icing sugar
raspberry jam

MIX muffin ingredients together until just combined. Three-quarters fill well-greased muffin pans and bake at 180°C for 15–20 minutes. Leave to cool. To make filling, mix chocolate, sour cream and icing sugar. Remove muffins from pans, make a diagonal cut into each, spread cuts thinly with raspberry jam and fill with frosting.

Black & White Muffins

50g butter, softened
1/2 cup caster sugar
1 egg
1 cup milk
2 cups flour
2 tsp baking powder
80g white chocolate, chopped
1 tblsp cocoa
80g dark chocolate, chopped

CREAM butter and sugar until fluffy. Add egg and milk, then mix in flour and baking powder until just combined. Divide mixture between two bowls. Add white chocolate to one, and to the other add cocoa and dark chocolate. Line muffin pans with paper cases and half fill each with white mixture, then top with dark mixture. Bake at 190°C for 20 minutes.

Blackberry Muffins

³/₄ cup natural yoghurt
¹/₂ cup water
2 eggs
2 cups blackberries (fresh, frozen or canned)
3 cups flour
1 tblsp baking powder
¹/₂ tsp baking soda
1 ¹/₂ cups sugar
icing sugar for dusting

IF using canned blackberries, reserve juice from berries and use ¹/₂ cup of this in place of water. Mix yoghurt, water or juice and eggs. Add remaining ingredients and mix until just combined. Spoon into well-greased muffin pans and bake at 180°C for 15–20 minutes. Dust with icing sugar just before serving.

Blackberry & Lemon Muffins

1 cup blackberries (fresh or frozen)
1/3 cup caster sugar
2 cups wholemeal flour
1 tblsp baking powder
1/2 tsp baking soda
2 tsp grated lemon peel
1 egg
1 1/4 cups buttermilk
3 tblsp oil

IN food processor fitted with metal blade, chop blackberries. Set aside in a bowl and mix with sugar. In large bowl, mix together flour, baking powder, baking soda and lemon peel. In a third bowl, beat the egg, buttermilk and oil. Add blackberries and wet ingredients to dry ingredients. Stir until everything is just moistened. Spoon into prepared muffin pans. Bake in a preheated 190°C oven for 15–20 minutes.

Blueberry Muffins

125g butter
2 3/4 cups flour
1 tsp salt
4 tsp baking powder
3/4 cup caster sugar
4 eggs
1 cup milk
2 cups blueberries, fresh or frozen
extra caster sugar

MELT butter and cool. Sift flour, salt, baking powder and sugar. Beat eggs until thick and fluffy. Whisk in milk and melted butter. Add egg mixture to dry ingredients, then fold in blueberries. Stir to just combine. Three-quarters fill greased muffin pans and sprinkle with caster sugar. Bake at 200°C for about 15 minutes.

Blueberry Fat-free Muffins

1 ³/₄ cups rolled oats
¹/₂ cup oat bran
³/₄ tsp baking soda
¹/₂ tsp cinnamon
³/₄ cup unsweetened apple sauce
¹/₂ cup honey
1 tsp vanilla essence
¹/₂ cup non-fat milk
3 egg whites, lightly beaten
1 cup blueberries

PULSE rolled oats and oat bran in food processor for 10 seconds. Reserve 2 tblsp oat mixture. In medium bowl, combine remaining oat mixture, baking soda and cinnamon; mix well and set aside. In small bowl, combine apple sauce, honey, vanilla and milk; pour into oat mixture. Stir until just blended. Gently mix in egg whites. Dust well-drained blueberries with 2 tblsp reserved oat mixture; gently fold the blueberries into batter. Divide mixture evenly into greased muffin pans and bake at 180°C for 20–25 minutes.

Brazil Nut & Fruit Muffins

2 cups flour
²/₃ cup brown sugar, packed
2 tsp baking powder
¹/₂ tsp salt
1 cup chopped dried apricots
³/₄ cup boiling water
¹/₂ cup oil
¹/₂ cup mashed banana
1 egg
1 tsp vanilla essence
1 cup chopped brazil nuts

IN large bowl mix together flour, brown sugar, baking powder and salt. In separate bowl combine apricots and boiling water and allow to soak for five minutes. Stir oil, banana, egg and vanilla into apricots. Make a well in centre of dry ingredients and add apricot mixture. Stir to combine, then fold in nuts. Spoon batter into prepared muffin pans and bake at 200°C for 16–20 minutes. Serve with butter while still warm.

Broccoli Cheese Muffins

1 egg
$^3/_4$ cup water
1 cup flour
1 tsp salt
1 tblsp baking powder
$^1/_2$ tsp cracked pepper
1 $^1/_2$ cups grated cheese
1 cup broccoli florets, steamed

MIX all ingredients together until just combined. Spoon into well-greased muffin pans and bake at 200°C for 12–15 minutes.

Brown Rice Muffins

1 1/4 cups wholemeal flour
1 1/2 tsp baking powder
1/2 tsp baking soda
1 tsp cinnamon
1 egg
3/4 cup buttermilk
1/4 cup maple syrup, golden syrup or honey
1 cup cooked brown rice (cool before using)
1/4 cup chopped raisins
3 tblsp oil

IN large bowl mix together flour, baking powder, baking soda and cinnamon. In separate bowl, whisk together egg, buttermilk and maple or golden syrup. Stir in rice, raisins and oil. Pour wet ingredients over dry ingredients and stir until just moistened. Divide batter between 16 lightly greased or paper-lined muffin pans. Bake in a preheated 190°C oven for 15–20 minutes. Let cool for 5 minutes before removing from the pans.

Cabbage, Frank & Tomato Muffins

2 cups cabbage, finely sliced
1 clove garlic, crushed
1 tsp brown sugar
1 tblsp oil
1 egg
³/₄ cup water
2 cups self-raising flour
¹/₂ tsp salt
2 frankfurters, chopped
2 tomatoes, chopped

GENTLY fry cabbage with garlic, sugar and oil until soft and browned. Transfer to a bowl. Add remaining ingredients and mix until just combined. Spoon into well-greased muffin pans and bake at 190°C for 15 minutes.

Cappuccino Chip Muffins

2 cups flour
³/₄ cup sugar
2 ¹/₂ tsp baking powder
2 tsp instant coffee
¹/₂ tsp salt
¹/₂ tsp ground cinnamon
1 cup milk
125g butter, melted and cooled slightly
1 egg
1 tsp vanilla essence
³/₄ cup chocolate chips
grated chocolate for sprinkling
Filling
100g cream cheese, 1 tblsp sugar, ¹/₂ tsp vanilla essence, ¹/₂ tsp coffee powder

IN large bowl mix together flour, sugar, baking powder, coffee, salt and cinnamon. In separate bowl mix together milk, butter, egg and vanilla. Make a well in centre of dry ingredients and add milk mixture. Stir to combine, then fold in chocolate chips. Spoon batter into prepared muffin tins and bake at 190ºC for 15–20 minutes. Cut in half, spread with filling and sprinkle with grated chocolate. To make filling, cream ingredients together.

Caramelised Onion Muffins

2 onions, thinly sliced
1 tblsp butter
1 tblsp sugar
1 egg, lightly beaten
1 cup self-raising flour
1/2 tsp salt
1/2 tsp cracked pepper
1 1/2 cups grated cheese

SLOWLY fry onions with butter and sugar until soft and golden. Transfer to a bowl. Make egg up to 1 cup with water and add with remaining ingredients to onion mixture. Mix until just combined. Spoon into well-greased muffin pans and bake at 190°C for 12–15 minutes.

Caraway & Cheese Muffins

2 cups flour
1 tblsp baking powder
$^1/_4$ tsp salt
1 tsp dried mustard
1 cup grated cheese
1 tblsp caraway seeds
1 egg
$^3/_4$ cup milk
50g butter, melted

SIFT flour, baking powder and salt. Stir in mustard, grated cheese and caraway seeds. Combine egg and milk. Stir melted butter, egg and milk into dry ingredients until just combined. Three-quarters fill greased muffin pans and bake at 200°C for 15–20 minutes.

Cardamom Muffins

1 ¹/₂ cups self-raising flour
pinch salt
1 tsp ground cardamom
¹/₄ cup sugar
1 egg
50g butter, melted
¹/₃ cup sour cream

SIFT flour, salt and cardamom and stir in sugar. Beat egg, melted butter and sour cream. Pour onto dry ingredients and mix until just combined. Three-quarters fill greased muffin pans and bake at 200°C for 15–20 minutes.

Carrot, Bacon & Parsley Muffins

2 cups flour
4 tsp baking powder
1 cup grated cheese
1 grated onion
1 cup grated carrot
chopped parsley
2 tblsp bacon bits
1 egg
1 large tblsp butter, melted
1 cup milk

SIFT flour and baking powder. Add cheese, onion, carrot, parsley and bacon bits. Beat egg; add melted butter and milk. Mix until just combined. Three-quarters fill greased muffin pans and bake at 200°C for 15–20 minutes.

Carrot Cake Muffins

1 3/4 cups flour
2/3 cup firmly packed light brown sugar
1 tsp baking powder
1/2 tsp baking soda
1/2 tsp salt
1 tsp ground cinnamon
dash ground mace
1/2 cup crushed pineapple in juice
1/2 cup vegetable oil
1 egg, lightly beaten
1 1/2 tsp vanilla essence
2 cups shredded carrot
1/2 cup raisins

IN large bowl, mix flour, brown sugar, baking powder, baking soda, salt, cinnamon and mace. In separate bowl, mix pineapple, oil, egg and vanilla until blended. Make a well in centre of dry ingredients; add pineapple mixture and stir to just combine. Stir in carrot and raisins. Spoon batter into prepared muffin pans and bake at 200°C for 15–20 minutes.

Carrot & Ginger Muffins

2 cups flour
1 tblsp baking powder
$^1/_4$ tsp ground ginger
$^1/_4$ cup brown sugar
$^3/_4$ cup grated carrot
$^1/_4$ cup crystallized ginger
1 egg
$^3/_4$ cup milk
50g butter, melted

S IFT flour, baking powder and ground ginger. Stir in sugar, carrot and crystallized ginger. Combine egg and milk, and add melted butter. Make a well in centre of dry ingredients and pour in milk and butter. Stir quickly until just combined. Three-quarters fill greased muffin pans and bake at 200°C for 20 minutes.

Cheese Muffins

2 cups flour
3 tsp baking powder
$^1/_4$ tsp salt
$^1/_2$ tsp dry mustard
freshly ground black pepper
2 cups grated tasty cheese
2 eggs
1 cup milk

S IFT flour, baking powder, salt, mustard and freshly ground
pepper. Add grated cheese. Lightly beat eggs and milk
together. Add eggs and milk to dry ingredients and mix together
lightly until just combined. Three-quarters fill greased muffin pans
and bake at 200°C for 10–15 minutes or until golden brown.

Cheese & Chive Muffins

1 egg
³/₄ cup water
1 cup self-raising flour
¹/₂ tsp salt
1 ¹/₂ cups grated cheese
1 tblsp fresh chives
coarse sea salt (optional)

MIX all ingredients together until just combined. Spoon into well-greased muffin pans and sprinkle with sea salt. Bake at 190°C for 15 minutes.

Cheese & Onion Muffins

$^1/_2$ *cup chopped onion*
1 tblsp melted butter
1 egg, lightly beaten
$^1/_2$ *cup milk*
1 $^1/_2$ cups self-raising flour
pinch salt
1 level tblsp butter
1 cup grated tasty cheese
1 tblsp poppy seeds
1 tblsp melted butter for drizzling

COOK onions in one tablespoon of melted butter until lightly brown. Mix beaten egg and milk together. Sift flour and salt. Rub in one tablespoon of butter. Mix dry ingredients with egg and milk to make a light scone batter. Add onions and half the cheese. Place small rounds in greased muffin pans and sprinkle with reamaining grated cheese and poppy seeds. Drizzle melted butter over top of muffins. Bake at 220°C for 15 minutes.

Cheese & Tomato Layer Muffins

1 egg
³/₄ cup water
2 cups self-raising flour
¹/₂ tsp salt
1 ¹/₂ cups grated cheddar
³/₄ cup commercial tomato pasta sauce

COMBINE all ingredients except pasta sauce. Half fill prepared muffin pans with mixture. Put up to 2 teaspoons pasta sauce in the middle of each muffin. Take care that sauce stays mostly in the middle. If there is too much sauce, muffins will come apart when removed from pans. Cover each muffin with remaining mixture until pans are three-quarters full. Bake at 200°C for 12–15 minutes.

Cherry Muffins

2 cups, plus 2 tblsp, flour
1 cup sugar
2 tsp baking powder
$^1/_4$ tsp salt
2 eggs, beaten
$^1/_2$ cup milk
$^1/_2$ cup butter or margarine, melted
1 tsp almond essence
2 cups fresh or canned pitted red cherries, drained
Topping
1–2 tblsp sugar
$^1/_4$ tsp ground nutmeg
1–2 tblsp sliced almonds

IN mixing bowl, stir together flour, sugar, baking powder and salt. Make a well in centre and set aside. In another bowl, combine eggs, milk, butter and essence. Add to flour mixture all at once; stir until just moistened. Gently fold in cherries. Spoon into well-greased muffin pans. Combine topping ingredients and sprinkle over batter. Bake at 190°C for 20–25 minutes.

Cherry & Walnut Muffins

2 cups flour
$^1/_3$ cup caster sugar
3 tsp baking powder
$^1/_4$ cup chopped glacé cherries
$^1/_3$ cup chopped walnuts
1 egg
1 cup milk
$^1/_4$ cup butter, melted
1 tsp vanilla essence

SIFT flour, sugar and baking powder, then add cherries and walnuts. Beat together egg, milk, melted butter and vanilla. Add to dry ingredients and mix gently until just combined. Three-quarters fill greased muffin pans and bake at 200°C for 15–20 minutes.

Chicken & Curry Muffins

1 1/4 cups flour
70g packet chicken soup
1 tblsp baking powder
1 tsp curry powder
3/4 cup milk
1 egg
50g butter, melted

SIFT flour and add soup mix, baking powder and curry powder. Combine milk and egg. Make a well in centre of dry ingredients. Pour in milk mixture and melted butter. Stir gently until just combined. Three-quarters fill greased muffin pans and bake at 200°C for 15–20 minutes.

Chilli Corn Muffins

1 finely chopped chilli or 1 tsp chilli powder
1 finely chopped small onion
1/4 cup oil
1 1/2 cups All-bran
1 1/2 cups Trim milk
2 egg whites
1 2/3 cups self-raising flour
1 x 325g can corn kernels, drained
1/2 cup grated tasty cheese
1 egg white, stiffly beaten

SAUTÉ chilli and onion in one tablespoon of oil until onion is tender. Cool. Place All-bran and milk in a bowl and stand for five minutes to soften. Stir in chilli mixture, remaining oil and two egg whites. Add flour, corn and 1/4 cup cheese. Finally, fold in remaining stiffly beaten egg white. Three-quarters fill greased muffin pans and sprinkle each muffin with a little of the remaining cheese. Bake at 190°C for 25–30 minutes.

Choc-Mallow Muffins

2 ³/₄ cups self-raising flour
¹/₄ cup cocoa
³/₄ cup brown sugar, firmly packed
¹/₂ cup white chocolate chips
¹/₂ cup dark chocolate chips
100g butter, melted and cooled slightly
1 egg, lightly beaten
1 ¹/₂ cups milk
Topping
150g dark chocolate, melted
2 tblsp butter, melted
¹/₂ cup chopped glacé cherries
³/₄ cup unsalted roasted peanuts
1 x 100g packet pink marshmallows

IN large bowl mix together sifted flour, cocoa, brown sugar, chocolate chips, butter, egg and milk. Spoon batter into prepared muffin pans and bake at 190°C for 20 minutes. To make topping, combine chocolate and butter, then stir in half the cherries and peanuts. Top muffins with this mixture and decorate with marshmallows and remaining cherries and peanuts.

Chocolate Muffins

150g fine cornmeal
$1/3$ cup self-raising flour
2 tblsp cocoa
1 tblsp baking powder
pinch of salt
$1/3$ cup dark brown sugar
60g butter, melted
$2/3$ cup sour cream
1 egg
2 tblsp strong black coffee
50g dark chocolate, broken into 12 pieces
cocoa for dusting

SIFT cornmeal, flour, cocoa, baking powder and salt into a bowl. Add brown sugar, then stir in butter, sour cream, egg and coffee. Spoon half the batter into prepared muffin pans. Place a piece of chocolate in each pan, then cover with remaining batter. Bake at 200°C for 20 minutes. Dust with cocoa before serving.

Chocolate Big Chip Muffins

2 cups flour
$1/3$ cup brown sugar, firmly packed
$1/3$ cup sugar
2 tsp baking powder
$1/2$ tsp salt
$2/3$ cup milk
2 eggs
125g butter, melted and cooled slightly
1 tsp vanilla essence
2 cups large chocolate chips or chunks
$1/2$ cup chopped pecans

IN large bowl mix together flour, sugars, baking powder and salt. In separate bowl mix together milk, eggs, butter and vanilla. Make a well in centre of dry ingredients and add milk mixture. Stir to combine, then fold in chocolate chips and pecans. Spoon batter into prepared muffin pans and bake at 200°C for 15–20 minutes. **Variation**: Serve iced with chocolate icing and sprinkled with chocolate chips and pecans.

Chocolate Bourbon Muffins

³/₄ cup flour
¹/₂ tsp baking soda
¹/₄ tsp salt
125g butter, softened
¹/₂ cup sugar
50g chocolate, melted and cooled slightly
1 egg
1 tblsp bourbon
1 tsp vanilla essence
¹/₂ cup chocolate chips
¹/₂ cup chopped pecans
icing sugar or cocoa for dusting

MIX together flour, baking soda and salt. In separate bowl cream butter and sugar until light and fluffy, then beat in chocolate, egg, bourbon and vanilla. Add dry ingredients and combine, then fold in chocolate chips and pecans. Spoon batter into prepared muffin pans and bake at 200°C for 15–20 minutes. Serve dusted with icing sugar or cocoa.

Chocolate Caramel Muffins

1 egg
75g soft butter
150g dark chocolate melted in 1 cup boiling water
2 cups flour
2 tsp baking powder
1 tblsp cocoa
1/2 cup caster sugar
Filling
1/2 x 400g can sweetened condensed milk
1 1/2 tsp butter
1 tblsp golden syrup

MIX all muffin ingredients together until just combined. Three-quarters fill well-greased muffin pans and bake at 180°C for 15–20 minutes. Leave to cool. To make filling, boil ingredients, stirring every 30 seconds, until they thicken into caramel. Take care as this mixture changes quickly. Remove muffins from pans, make a diagonal cut into each and fill with caramel.

Chocolate Cherry Brandy Muffins

1 egg
150g dark chocolate, melted in 1 cup boiling water
75g butter, softened
2 cups flour
2 tsp baking powder
1 tblsp cocoa
1/2 cup caster sugar
1 cup glacé cherries mixed with 1/4 cup brandy

MIX all ingredients together until just combined. Three-quarters fill prepared muffin pans and bake at 180°C for 15–20 minutes.

Chocolate Raspberry Muffins

1 x 425g can raspberries in syrup
2 cups self-raising flour
$^1/_2$ cup sugar
$^1/_2$ cup chocolate chips
1 egg
60g butter, melted and cooled slightly
$^3/_4$ cup buttermilk
Filling
1 x 300ml carton cream
2 tblsp cocoa
2 tblsp icing sugar
2 tblsp raspberry jam

PUT undrained raspberries in a saucepan and bring to boil. Simmer for 12 minutes, then allow to cool. In large bowl mix together flour, sugar and chocolate chips. In separate bowl mix together egg, butter and buttermilk. Make a well in centre of dry ingredients and add buttermilk mixture. Stir to combine, then fold in raspberry mixture. Spoon into prepared muffin pans and bake at 190°C for 15 minutes. To serve, split and add filling. To make filling, whip cream, cocoa and icing sugar together, then fold in jam.

Christmas Morning Cranberry Muffins

1 cup cranberries
$^1/_2$ cup sugar
1 $^1/_2$ cups flour
2 tsp baking powder
1 tsp salt
$^1/_2$ tsp ground cinnamon
$^1/_4$ tsp ground allspice
$^1/_4$ tsp ground nutmeg
1 egg, beaten
$^1/_4$ tsp grated orange rind
$^3/_4$ cup orange juice
75g butter, melted and cooled slightly
$^1/_4$ cup chopped nuts

CHOP cranberries coarsely and sprinkle with half the sugar. Set aside. In large bowl mix together remaining sugar, flour, baking powder, salt and spices. In separate bowl mix together egg, orange rind, orange juice and butter. Make a well in centre of dry ingredients and add orange mixture. Stir to moisten, then fold in cranberries and chopped nuts. Spoon batter into prepared muffin pans and bake at 190°C for 15–20 minutes.

Christmas Muffins

2 ¹/₂ cups sugar
4 cups flour
4 tsp cinnamon
4 tsp baking soda
1 tsp salt
1 cup raisins, plumped in brandy and drained
1 cup desiccated coconut
4 cups grated carrot
2 cups grated apple
1 cup pecans or walnuts, roughly chopped
6 eggs
2 cups vegetable oil
1 tsp vanilla essence
icing sugar for dusting

SIFT dry ingredients into large bowl. Lightly dust raisins with flour. Add coconut, carrot, apple and nuts, and stir well. Add eggs, oil and vanilla. Stir until combined. Spoon into deep muffin pans and bake at 190°C for 20 minutes. Serve dusted with icing sugar. Quantities can be halved.

Cinnamon Sugar Muffins

2 tsp ground cinnamon
$^2/_3$ cup sugar
2 cups self-raising flour
$^3/_4$ cup water
1 egg
2 tblsp golden syrup

MIX cinnamon and sugar together. Reserve one-third for topping and two-thirds for muffin centres. Mix remaining ingredients together until just combined. One-third fill well-greased muffin pans with mixture and sprinkle with two-thirds of the cinnamon sugar. Fill pans with remaining mixture and sprinkle with the rest of the cinnamon sugar. Bake at 200°C for 15 minutes.

Coconut Pineapple Muffins

2 cups flour
1 tblsp baking powder
$^1/_2$ tsp salt
$^1/_2$ cup sugar
$^1/_2$ cup coconut
1 egg
$^1/_4$ cup oil
$^1/_3$ cup milk
1 tsp vanilla essence
1 x 225g can crushed pineapple, drained
$^1/_2$ cup slivered almonds

IN large bowl mix together flour, baking powder, salt, sugar and coconut. In separate bowl mix together egg, oil, milk, vanilla and pineapple. Add to dry ingredients and stir until just moistened. Spoon batter into prepared muffin pans and sprinkle over slivered almonds. Bake at 200°C for 20 minutes.

Coffee Banana Muffins

50g butter
1/4 cup sugar
1 tsp instant coffee
1 tsp baking soda
1/3 cup warm milk
1 egg
2 bananas, mashed
1 cup flour
1 tsp baking powder
Icing
1 tsp instant coffee powder
1 tblsp boiling water
1 tsp butter
1 cup icing sugar

CREAM butter and sugar until fluffy. Dissolve coffee and baking soda in warm milk and stir into butter mixture. Add remaining ingredients and mix until just combined. Three-quarters fill well-greased muffin pans and bake at 160°C for 20–25 minutes. Leave to cool. To make icing, combine ingredients.

Coffee Walnut Muffins

1 tblsp instant coffee
1 cup hot water
$^1/_2$ cup milk or cream
1 egg, beaten
$^1/_2$ cup oil
1 $^1/_2$ cups flour
$^1/_3$ cup sugar
3 tsp baking powder
1 tsp salt
$^1/_2$ cup chopped walnuts
icing sugar for dusting

DISSOLVE coffee in hot water. Add milk or cream, egg and oil. In large bowl mix together flour, sugar, baking powder and salt, then add walnuts. Add milk mixture to dry ingredients and stir. Spoon batter into prepared muffin pans and bake at 190°C for 15–20 minutes. Serve dusted with icing sugar.

Coriander Corn Muffins

1 ¹/₂ cups flour
¹/₂ cup yellow cornmeal
¹/₄ cup sugar
¹/₄ cup brown sugar, packed
1 tsp baking powder
¹/₂ tsp ground coriander
¹/₄ tsp salt
¹/₂ cup Trim milk
¹/₄ cup oil
2 egg whites
1 cup corn kernels

IN large bowl, combine flour, cornmeal, sugar, brown sugar, baking powder, coriander and salt; mix well. In small bowl, combine milk, oil and egg whites; blend well. Add to flour mixture all at once; stir until dry ingredients are just moistened. Gently stir in corn. Spoon batter evenly into muffin pans. Bake at 200°C for 14–20 minutes, or until light golden brown.

Corn & Bacon Muffins

1 egg
2 cups flour
$^1/_2$ tsp salt
1 tblsp baking powder
1 cup creamed corn
1 cup grated cheese
2 rashers bacon, cooked and chopped

MAKE egg up to $^3/_4$ cup with water. Add remaining ingredients and mix until just combined. Spoon into prepared muffin pans and bake at 200°C for 15–20 minutes.

Corn & Pecan Muffins

3 ¹/₂ cups wholemeal flour
1 cup yellow cornmeal
1 sachet dry yeast
1 tsp baking powder
1 tsp salt
1 cup milk
100g butter
¹/₂ cup water
¹/₃ cup honey
2 eggs
1 cup chopped pecans
¹/₂ cup sultanas

COMBINE flour, cornmeal, yeast, baking powder and salt in a bowl. Heat milk, butter (cut up), water and honey to lukewarm. Beat eggs. Pour liquid and eggs over dry ingredients. Add nuts and sultanas and mix well. Knead on a board for a few minutes. Half fill greased muffin pans and leave in a warm place to rise. Bake at 200°C for 15–18 minutes or until firm.

Corn & Tomato Muffins

$^3/_4$ cup cornmeal
$^1/_2$ cup white flour
1 tblsp granulated sugar
3 tsp baking powder
$^1/_4$ tsp salt
$^2/_3$ cup Trim milk
1 egg white, lightly beaten
$^1/_2$ cup plum tomatoes, seeded and diced
1 tblsp fresh basil, minced
fresh oregano

S PRAY muffin pans with vegetable spray. In medium bowl, combine cornmeal, flour, sugar, baking powder and salt; set aside. In small bowl, combine milk, egg white, tomato and herbs. Pour into flour mixture, stirring until just combined. Spoon into muffin pans and bake at 200°C for 20 minutes.

Cottage Cheese & Cheddar Muffins

1 egg
³/₄ cup water
1 cup cottage cheese
1 cup self-raising flour
1 tsp salt
1 cup grated tasty cheese
2 tblsp grated Parmesan cheese

MIX together all ingredients except Parmesan until just combined. Spoon into well-greased muffin pans and sprinkle with Parmesan. Bake at 190°C for 12–15 minutes.

Cranberry & Apple Muffins

1 $\frac{1}{2}$ cups flour
1 tsp baking soda
1 tsp cinnamon
$\frac{1}{4}$ tsp salt
2 egg whites, whipped
$\frac{3}{4}$ cup brown sugar, packed
$\frac{1}{4}$ cup apple sauce
1 tsp vanilla essence
$\frac{3}{4}$ cup apple, peeled and chopped finely
$\frac{3}{4}$ cup cranberries, chopped

GREASE muffin pans and dust with flour. In mixing bowl, combine flour, baking soda, cinnamon and salt. In separate bowl, combine egg whites, brown sugar, apple sauce, vanilla, apple and cranberries. Mix dry ingredients with wet ingredients until just combined. Fill muffin pans three-quarters full. Bake at 180°C for 20–25 minutes, or until lightly browned.

Cranberry & Pecan Muffins

1 1/2 cups milk
2 eggs
75g butter, melted
1 cup wholemeal flour
1 cup flour
1/3 cup sugar
3 tsp baking powder
1/2 tsp salt
1 1/4 cups cranberry sauce
100g chopped pecans

COMBINE milk, eggs and melted butter. Beat briskly. Add remaining ingredients and stir until just combined. The batter should look lumpy. Three-quarters fill greased muffin pans and bake at 200°C for 20–25 minutes or until lightly browned.

Cream Cheese & Lemon Muffins

110g cream cheese
1 1/2 cups flour
grated rind of 1 lemon
1 egg
1/2 cup, plus 1 tsp, oil
1/2 cup milk
2/3 cup sugar
1 1/2 tsp baking powder
1/2 tsp salt
Topping
2 tblsp lemon juice (fresh)
1 tblsp sugar

CUT cream cheese into small pieces, mix with 2 tablespoons flour and grate the lemon rind into the mixture. Add rest of ingredients. Mix until just combined and spoon into greased muffin pans. Bake at 190°C for 20–25 minutes. To make topping, mix to form lemon sugar. Sprinkle over warm muffins.

Date Muffins

2 tblsp butter
¹/₄ cup brown sugar
2 eggs
1 cup milk
2 cups flour
1 tsp baking powder
pinch of salt
1 cup finely chopped dates

CREAM butter and sugar. Add eggs and milk, then sifted flour, baking powder and salt. Fold in finely chopped dates. Stir to just combine. Three-quarters fill greased muffin pans and bake at 200°C for 12–15 minutes.

Date & Bacon Muffins

$^1/_4$ cup butter, softened
2 tblsp sugar
1 egg
2 cups flour
1 tblsp baking powder
$^1/_2$ tsp salt
1 cup milk
$^3/_4$ cup dates, chopped
4 slices bacon, cooked and crumbled

CREAM butter; gradually add sugar, beating well. Add egg, beat until well combined. Combine dry ingredients; add to creamed mix alternately with milk, beginning and ending with dry ingredients. Stir in dates and crumbled bacon. Spoon batter into greased muffin pans, filling two-thirds full. Bake at 200°C for 20 minutes.

Date & Orange Muffins

1 orange, peeled and quartered
1/2 cup orange juice
1 egg
100g butter, melted
1 1/2 cups flour
1 tsp baking powder
1/4 tsp salt
1 tsp baking soda
3/4 cup sugar
1/2 cup chopped dates

PLACE orange in food processor and process until pulp. Add orange juice, egg and melted butter, and combine. Sift flour, baking powder, salt, baking soda and sugar. Add mixture from processor to dry ingredients. Add chopped dates and mix until just combined. Three-quarters fill greased muffin pans and bake at 190°C for 15 minutes or until cooked.

Date & Walnut Muffins

1 tsp baking soda
1 cup chopped dates
³/₄ cup boiling water
2 eggs
1 cup brown sugar
1 tsp vanilla essence
1 ¹/₂ cups flour
¹/₂ tsp salt
2 tsp baking powder
¹/₂ cup roughly chopped walnuts

S PRINKLE baking soda over dates, pour over boiling water and leave to cool. Whisk eggs, sugar and vanilla and mix into cooled date mix. Add dry ingredients and mix until just combined. Spoon into well-greased muffin pans and bake at 180°C for 18 minutes.

Deerfield Spice Muffins

200g raisin bran cereal
1 $\frac{1}{2}$ cups sugar
2 $\frac{1}{2}$ cups flour
2 $\frac{1}{2}$ tsp baking soda
1 tsp salt
$\frac{1}{2}$ tsp ground cinnamon
$\frac{1}{2}$ tsp ground cloves
$\frac{1}{2}$ tsp ground nutmeg
2 eggs
$\frac{1}{2}$ cup oil
475ml buttermilk (or yoghurt)
1 tsp vanilla essence

MIX dry ingredients in large bowl. Stir in remaining ingredients. Mix well. Fill muffin pans two-thirds full. Bake at 200°C for 15 minutes.

Dilly Zucchini Ricotta Muffins

1 1/2 cups flour
2 tblsp sugar
3 tsp baking powder
1/2 tsp salt
3/4 tsp dill
1/4 cup milk
1/2 cup margarine or butter, melted
2 large eggs
2/3 cup ricotta cheese
1/2 cup shredded zucchini

IN large bowl, combine flour, sugar, baking powder, salt and dill; mix well. In medium bowl combine milk, margarine and eggs. Stir in ricotta cheese and zucchini; beat well. Add to dry ingredients, stirring until just moistened (batter will be stiff). Fill prepared muffin pans two-thirds full. Bake at 200°C for 20–25 minutes or until golden brown.

Dotty Pumpkin Muffins

60g butter, melted and cooled slightly
$^1/_4$ cup brown sugar
1 egg
1 cup mashed cooked pumpkin
$^1/_2$ cup milk
1 cup chocolate chips or chunks
2 cups self-raising flour
1 tsp baking powder
1 tsp ground cinnamon
chocolate chips for sprinkling

IN large bowl mix together butter, sugar, egg, pumpkin and milk. Add chocolate chips, flour, baking powder and cinnamon and stir until just combined. Spoon batter into prepared muffin pans and bake at 180°C for 18–20 minutes. Sprinkle with chocolate chips. If desired, spread with cream cheese icing first.

Double Chocolate Muffins

¹/4 cup cocoa
¹/4 cup boiling water
3 cups flour
1 ¹/2 tblsp baking powder
³/4 cup sugar
1 cup chocolate chips
1 egg, beaten
1 ¹/2 cups evaporated milk
125g butter, melted and cooled slightly
icing sugar or cocoa for dusting

MIX cocoa and boiling water together to make a smooth paste. Allow to cool. Sift flour, baking powder and sugar into a large bowl and add chocolate chips. In separate bowl mix together cocoa mixture, egg, evaporated milk and butter. Make a well in centre of dry ingredients and add milk mixture. Stir until just combined. Spoon batter into prepared muffin pans and bake at 190°C for 20 minutes. Serve dusted with icing sugar or cocoa.

Doughnut-Flavoured Muffins

1 3/4 cups flour
1 1/2 tsp baking powder
1/2 tsp salt
1/4 tsp ground cinnamon
1/2 tsp ground nutmeg
1/3 cup oil
3/4 cup sugar
1 egg
3/4 cup milk
Topping
1/2 cup melted butter
3/4 cup sugar
1 tsp ground cinnamon

IN large bowl mix together flour, baking powder, salt and spices. In separate bowl mix together oil, sugar, egg and milk. Add oil mixture to dry ingredients and stir to combine. Spoon batter into prepared muffin pans and bake at 190ºC for 20 minutes. Remove from pans while still warm and brush with melted butter, then sprinkle with sugar and cinnamon mixed together. **Variation**: Half fill muffin pans with batter. Add 1 tsp raspberry jam in each pan and cover with rest of batter.

Egg & Tuna Muffins

1 x 185g can of tuna in water, drained and flaked (reserve liquid)
1 egg
1 cup flour
1 tsp salt
1 tblsp baking powder
1 cup grated mild cheese
2 hard-boiled eggs, sliced lengthways

MAKE up liquid from tuna to ³/₄ cup with water and mix with tuna, egg, flour, salt, baking powder and cheese until just combined. Three-quarters fill well-greased muffin pans and bake at 200°C for 12–15 minutes. Leave to cool for five minutes. Make a small diagonal split in top of each muffin and insert two slices of hard-boiled egg.

Extra Fibre Muffins

1 ¹/₄ cups flour
¹/₂ cup sugar
1 tblsp baking powder
2 cups All bran
1 ¹/₄ cups Trim milk
1 egg
¹/₄ cup apple sauce

STIR together flour, sugar and baking powder. In large mixing bowl combine cereal and milk. Let stand 5 minutes or until cereal softens. Add egg and apple sauce. Beat well. Add flour mixture, stirring until just combined. Three-quarters fill muffin pans and bake at 200°C for 20 minutes until lightly brown.

Fresh Fruit Muffins

2 cups flour
4 tsp baking powder
$^1/_2$ tsp salt
$^1/_2$ cup caster sugar
100g butter, melted and cooled slightly
1 cup milk
1 egg
1–1 $^1/_2$ cups chopped fresh fruit
1 cup chopped walnuts
1 tblsp sugar for sprinkling
$^1/_2$ tsp ground cinnamon for sprinkling

IN large bowl mix together flour, baking powder, salt and sugar. In separate bowl mix together melted butter, milk and egg. Add milk mixture to dry ingredients, followed by prepared fruit and walnuts. Stir to combine. Spoon into prepared muffin pans and sprinkle with sugar and cinnamon mixed together. Bake at 200°C for 15 minutes. Split and serve with butter. **Variation**: Serve with yoghurt mixed with the appropriate fruit. Also good with whipped cream.

Fresh Ginger Muffins

50g piece ginger root
1 cup sugar
2 tblsp lemon zest
$^1/_2$ cup butter or margarine, softened
2 eggs
1 cup buttermilk (or yoghurt)
2 cups flour
$^1/_2$ tsp salt
$^3/_4$ tsp baking soda

FINELY chop unpeeled ginger. Put ginger and $^1/_4$ cup sugar in pan and cook over medium heat until sugar has melted. Let mixture cool. Chop lemon zest into small bits and stir in $^1/_4$ cup sugar. Add lemon mixture to ginger mixture. Stir and set aside. Put butter in bowl with remaining $^1/_2$ cup sugar and beat until smooth. Add eggs and buttermilk and mix well. Add flour, salt, baking soda and ginger-lemon mixture and mix until just combined. Three-quarters fill prepared muffin pans and bake at 190°C for 15–20 minutes. Serve warm.

Fresh Raspberry Muffins

2 cups flour
$^3/_4$ tsp baking soda
$^3/_4$ tsp cinnamon
$^1/_4$ tsp freshly grated nutmeg
$^1/_4$ tsp ground ginger
$^1/_4$ tsp salt
1 cup sugar
2 large eggs
2 tsp vanilla essence
$^1/_2$ cup oil
4 tblsp melted butter, cooled
1 cup fresh raspberries

BLEND together flour, baking soda, cinnamon, nutmeg, ginger and salt in large mixing bowl. Whisk sugar and eggs in small bowl until light. Blend in vanilla, oil and butter. Make a large well in centre of dry ingredients, pour in egg-sugar mixture and combine the two mixtures quickly until batter is formed. Gently fold in raspberries. Spoon batter into prepared muffin pans, filling them two-thirds full. Bake at 200°C for 20–22 minutes.

Fruit Mincemeat Muffins

2 cups flour
$1/3$ cup sugar
2 tsp baking powder
$1/2$ tsp salt
1 $1/4$ cups prepared fruit mincemeat
2 eggs, beaten
$1/3$ cup water
$1/3$ cup oil
1 tsp vanilla essence
1 cup chopped walnuts
Filling
raspberry jam
whipped cream

IN large bowl mix together flour, sugar, baking powder and salt. In separate bowl mix together mincemeat, eggs, water, oil and vanilla. Make a well in centre of dry ingredients and add mincemeat mixture. Stir to combine, then fold in walnuts. Spoon batter into prepared muffin pans and bake at 200°C for 20 minutes. To serve, cut in half and spread with raspberry jam and a dollop of freshly whipped cream.

Fruit Salad Muffins

2 eggs
1 x 400–450g can fruit salad in juice, drained (juice reserved)
³/₄ cup juice from fruit
100g butter, melted
2 cups self-raising flour
¹/₂ cup sugar

MIX all ingredients together until just combined. Spoon into well-greased muffin pans and bake at 180°C for 15–20 minutes.

Fruit Yoghurt Muffins

1 egg
³/₄ cup water
150g fruit-flavoured yoghurt
50g butter, melted
2 cups flour
1 tblsp baking powder
¹/₂ cup sugar

MIX all ingredients until just combined. Three-quarters fill well-greased muffin pans and bake at 180°C for 15–20 minutes.

Fruity Muffins

75g butter
1 egg, beaten
1 cup milk
1–1 ¹/₂ cups fruit (peaches, pineapple, blueberries, apricots,
strawberries) cut into small cubes
2 cups flour
4 tsp baking powder
¹/₂ tsp salt
¹/₂ cup caster sugar
Topping
1 tblsp sugar
¹/₂ tsp cinnamon

MELT butter, add egg and milk and beat to combine. Add with fruit to sifted dry ingredients. Don't overmix. Spoon into greased muffin pans and sprinkle with topping. Bake at 220°C for 15–20 minutes.

Fruity Bran Muffins

1 1/4 cups All-bran
3/4 cup Trim milk
1 egg
1/4 cup oil
1/4 cup raw sugar
1 3/4 cups self-raising flour
1 tsp cinnamon
2/3 cup mixed dried fruit
1 egg white
extra All-bran for topping

PLACE All-bran and milk in bowl and let stand for five minutes to soften. Beat egg, oil and sugar together and add to All-bran. Sift flour and add to All-bran with cinnamon and mixed fruit. Mix until just combined. Do not overmix. Fold in stiffly beaten egg white. Three-quarters fill greased muffin pans and sprinkle each muffin with some extra All-bran. Bake at 190°C for 25–30 minutes or until cooked.

Fudge-Filled Peanut Butter Muffins

$^1/_2$ cup chocolate chips
1 tblsp unsalted butter
1 $^2/_3$ cups flour
1 tblsp baking powder
$^1/_2$ cup brown sugar, firmly packed
$^1/_4$ tsp salt
$^3/_4$ cup milk
$^1/_2$ cup peanut butter
$^1/_3$ cup oil
1 egg, beaten
1 $^1/_2$ tsp vanilla essence
$^1/_2$ cup chopped salted peanuts

IN small saucepan heat chocolate chips and butter until melted, reserve. In large bowl mix together flour, baking powder, sugar and salt. In separate bowl mix together milk, peanut butter, oil, egg and vanilla until well combined. Make a well in centre of dry ingredients and add milk mixture. Stir to combine. Spoon half the batter into prepared muffin pans. Put a spoonful of melted chocolate mixture on top, making sure it does not touch the sides. Cover with remaining batter. Sprinkle over chopped peanuts and bake at 200°C for 15–20 minutes.

Garden Herb Muffins

2 cups flour
1 tblsp granulated sugar
2 tsp baking powder
1 tsp garlic powder
1 tsp dry mustard
$^1/_2$ tsp salt
2 egg whites, lightly beaten
1 cup Trim milk
$^1/_2$ cup grated carrot
$^1/_4$ cup chopped green onion
2 tblsp olive oil
2 tblsp non-fat plain yoghurt

INTO large bowl, sift together flour and the next five dry ingredients. In small mixing bowl, combine egg and remaining ingredients. Blend egg mixture gently into flour mixture. Spoon batter into prepared muffin pans. Bake at 190°C for 18–20 minutes.

Ginger Muffins

1 cup milk
50g butter
1 tblsp golden syrup
1 tsp baking soda
1 egg, lightly beaten
1 cup oat bran
1/2 cup sugar
2 tblsp chopped crystallized ginger
1 tsp ground ginger
1 cup flour
1/2 cup rolled oats
1/2 tsp salt

HEAT milk, butter and golden syrup until butter melts. Add baking soda and egg. In bowl, mix oat bran, sugar, crystallized and ground ginger, flour, rolled oats and salt. Add milk mixture and mix until only just combined. Three-quarters fill greased muffin pans and bake at 200°C for 10–15 minutes.

Ginger Peach Muffins

1 egg
$^1/_4$ cup milk
75g butter, melted
1 $^1/_2$ cups chopped peach slices (juice reserved)
$^1/_2$ cup juice from peaches
2 cups flour
1 tblsp baking powder
1 tsp ground ginger
$^1/_2$ cup sugar
$^1/_2$ cup crystallized ginger, finely chopped

MIX all ingredients until just combined. Spoon into well-greased muffin pans and bake at 180°C for 15 minutes.

Ginger Pear Muffins

2 cups flour
$^1/_2$ cup brown sugar, firmly packed
1 tsp baking soda
$^1/_2$ tsp salt
2 tsp ground ginger
1 tsp ground cinnamon
pinch each of ground nutmeg, ground cloves
1 cup natural yoghurt
$^1/_2$ cup oil
3 tblsp molasses
1 egg, beaten
1 $^1/_2$ cups diced pears
$^1/_2$ cup raisins
$^1/_4$ cup chopped walnuts

IN large bowl mix together flour, brown sugar, baking soda, salt and spices. In separate bowl mix together yoghurt, oil, molasses and egg. Make a well in centre of dry ingredients and add yoghurt mixture. Stir to combine, then fold in pears, raisins and walnuts. Spoon batter into prepared muffin pans and bake at 200°C for 20 minutes. Serve warm with butter. **Variation**: Top with ginger icing, made from 1$^1/_2$ cups icing sugar, 1 tsp ground ginger, 1 tblsp butter and boiling water to mix.

Ginger Pineapple Muffins

2 eggs
1 cup milk
100g butter, melted
1 x 440g can crushed pineapple, drained
1 cup white flour
1 cup wholemeal flour
1 tblsp baking powder
$^1/_2$ cup bran
2 tsp ground ginger
$^1/_2$ cup brown sugar

MIX all ingredients together until just combined. Three-quarters fill greased muffin pans and bake at 180°C for 15–20 minutes. **Hint**: Up to half the milk can be replaced by the liquid from the pineapple if it is in juice. Don't use if it is syrup.

Gingerbread & Lemon-Iced Muffins

1 1/4 cups flour
1/2 cup wholemeal flour
1/2 cup brown sugar, firmly packed
1 tsp baking soda
1/4 tsp salt
2 tsp ground ginger
1 tsp ground cinnamon
1/8 tsp ground cloves
1/8 tsp ground nutmeg
3/4 cup buttermilk
1/2 cup oil
2 eggs, beaten
1/4 cup molasses
1 cup currants
Glaze
3/4 cup icing sugar
2 tsp lemon juice

IN large bowl mix together flours, sugar, baking soda, salt and spices. In separate bowl mix together buttermilk, oil, eggs and molasses. Make a well in centre of dry ingredients and add buttermilk mixture. Stir to combine, then fold in currants. Spoon batter into prepared muffin pans and bake at 200°C for 15–20 minutes. To serve, beat icing sugar and lemon juice and drizzle over muffins.

Gingery Lemon Muffins

1/4 cup margarine, at room temperature
1/4 cup sugar
1 egg
2 tblsp peeled and coarsely chopped ginger root
2 tblsp grated lemon peel
1 tsp baking soda
1 1/2 cups plain, low-fat yoghurt or buttermilk
2 cups plain flour

IN large bowl, cream together margarine and sugar. Beat in egg. Add ginger and lemon peel. In separate small bowl, stir baking soda into buttermilk; it will start to bubble and rise. Fold flour into ginger mixture one third at a time, alternating with buttermilk. When well blended, spoon into greased muffin pans. Bake in a preheated 190°C oven for 15–20 minutes, or until lightly browned.

Goat Cheese & Pesto Muffins

$^1/_2$ cup pesto
$^3/_4$ cup water
1 egg
2 cups flour
$^1/_2$ tsp salt
1 tblsp baking powder
100g goat cheese, crumbled or cubed
1 cup grated cheddar

STIR pesto into water, then mix with remaining ingredients until just combined. Spoon into well-greased muffin pans and bake at 200°C for 12–15 minutes.

Golden Medley Muffins

Bowl 1: 1 cup white flour
1 cup wholemeal flour
$1/2$ cup oatmeal
2 tsp baking soda
2 tsp cinnamon
$1/2$ tsp allspice
$1/4$ tsp cardamom
$1/2$ tsp salt
Bowl 2: 1 cup raisins
1 cup shredded apple
$1/2$ cup shredded zucchini
$1/2$ cup shredded carrot
$1/2$ cup coconut
$1/2$ cup finely chopped pecans
Bowl 3: $1/2$ cup oil
1 cup honey
2 eggs, beaten
2 tsp vanilla essence

PREHEAT oven to 180°C. Mix all dry ingredients in bowl 1. Mix fruit, vegetables and nuts in bowl 2. Mix wet ingredients in bowl 3. Add contents of bowl 3 to bowl 1. Mix until moist. Fold in contents of bowl 2. Three-quarters fill prepared muffin pans. Sprinkle pecans or oatmeal on top if desired. Bake 25–30 minutes.

Great Guava Muffins

1 egg
$1/4$ cup milk
$1/2$ cup water
75g butter, melted
2 cups flour
1 tblsp baking powder
$1/3$ cup sugar
$1 1/2$ cups canned guavas, drained and roughly chopped

MIX all ingredients until just combined. Spoon into well-greased muffin pans and bake at 180°C for 15 minutes. **Hint**: Fresh guavas can be used – gently peel off skin and increase sugar to $1/2$ cup.

Ham & Cheese Muffins

1 egg, beaten
1 cup flour
1 tblsp baking powder
1 cup grated cheese
$^1/_2$ cup crumbled blue cheese
1 cup chopped ham

MAKE egg up to 1 cup with water and mix with remaining ingredients until just combined. Three-quarters fill well-greased muffin pans and bake at 200°C for 12–15 minutes.

Hazelnut Praline Muffins

$^1/_2$ cup chopped hazelnuts
$^1/_2$ cup sugar
$^1/_3$ cup oil
$^3/_4$ cup sugar
1 egg
$^3/_4$ cup milk
1 $^3/_4$ cups flour
1 $^1/_2$ tsp baking powder

GENTLY boil hazelnuts and first measure of sugar until mixture turns golden brown. Pour onto greased tinfoil and leave to set. Break praline into small pieces and crush with rolling pin or in food processor. Whisk oil, second measure of sugar, egg and milk together, then add dry ingredients and praline, mixing until just combined. Spoon into well-greased muffin pans and bake at 190°C for 20 minutes.

Hazelnut Spiced Muffins

2 cups flour
2 tsp baking powder
$^1/_2$ tsp salt
1 tsp ground cinnamon
$^1/_8$ tsp ground cloves
125g butter, softened
$^1/_2$ cup brown sugar, firmly packed
$^1/_4$ cup sugar
1 egg, beaten
1 tsp grated lemon rind
$^1/_2$ tsp vanilla essence
1 cup milk
$^3/_4$ cup ground or very finely chopped hazelnuts
$^1/_4$ cup raspberry jam

IN large bowl mix together flour, baking powder, salt, cinnamon and cloves. In separate bowl cream butter and sugars until light and fluffy, then beat in egg, lemon rind, vanilla and milk. Make a well in centre of dry ingredients and add butter mixture. Stir to combine, then fold in hazelnuts. Spoon half the batter into prepared muffin pans. Put a spoonful of raspberry jam on top, then cover with remaining batter. Bake at 200°C for 15–20 minutes. Sprinkle with sugar and cinnamon mixed together.

High Protein Muffins

2 ¹/₂ cups bran flakes
1 ¹/₂ cups raisins
1 ³/₄ cups milk
1 cup wholemeal flour
1 cup soy flour
1 cup toasted wheatgerm
4 tsp baking powder
1 ¹/₂ tsp ground nutmeg
³/₄ tsp salt
4 large eggs, lightly beaten
²/₃ cup honey
²/₃ cup oil
¹/₄ cup dark molasses

COMBINE bran flakes, raisins and milk in large mixing bowl. Stir together wholemeal flour, soy flour, wheatgerm, baking powder, nutmeg and salt; set aside. Combine eggs, honey, oil and molasses in small bowl; blend well. Add egg mixture to soaked bran flakes; mix well. Add dry ingredients to bran mixture, stirring to just moisten. Spoon batter into prepared muffin pans, filling three-quarters full. Bake at 180°C for 25 minutes or until golden brown.

Hokey-Pokey Muffins

$1/2$ cup sugar
1 tblsp water
2 tsp vinegar
$1/4$ cup golden syrup
$1/2$ tsp baking soda
$1/3$ cup oil
$3/4$ cup sugar
1 egg
$3/4$ cup milk
1 $1/2$ cups flour
1 $1/2$ tsp baking powder

GENTLY heat first measure of sugar with water and vinegar until sugar dissolves. Add golden syrup and continue cooking until a drop of the mixture forms a brittle ball when dropped in cold water. Remove from heat, add baking soda and stir gently while mixture froths. Pour onto greased tinfoil, leave to set, then break into very small pieces. Whisk oil, sugar, egg and milk together. Add hokey-pokey pieces and remaining ingredients and mix until just combined. Three-quarters fill well-greased muffin pans and bake at 190°C for 20 minutes.

Honey Bran Muffins

1 1/4 cups wholemeal flour
1 1/4 cups wheat bran
2 tsp baking powder
1/2 tsp baking soda
1 1/4 cups buttermilk
1/4 cup honey
1 egg
2 tblsp vegetable oil

IN large mixing bowl, combine flour, bran, baking powder and soda. Mix thoroughly. In small bowl, beat together buttermilk, honey, egg and oil. Pour wet ingredients over dry ingredients and stir until just moistened. Spoon batter into prepared muffin pans. Bake in a preheated 190°C oven for 15–20 minutes, or until lightly browned and muffins spring back to the touch. Cool slightly before serving.

Honey & Date Muffins

75g butter
$^1/_2$ cup honey
1 $^1/_2$ cups chopped dates
2 eggs
$^1/_4$ cup milk
1 $^1/_2$ cups flour
2 tsp baking powder

HEAT butter and honey only long enough to melt butter. Stir in chopped dates. Beat eggs with milk. Sift flour and baking powder. Make a well in centre of flour and add honey and egg mixtures. Mix until dry ingredients are just moistened. Three-quarters fill greased muffin pans and bake at 200°C for 15–20 minutes or until cooked.

Hot Cross Muffins

2 cups flour
$^3/_4$ cup sugar
2 tsp baking powder
$^1/_2$ tsp salt
$^1/_4$ tsp ground cinnamon
$^1/_8$ tsp ground allspice
1 cup milk
125g butter, melted and cooled slightly
1 egg, beaten
1 tsp vanilla essence
$^1/_2$ tsp grated orange rind
$^1/_4$ tsp grated lemon rind
1 cup currants
Glaze
$^1/_3$ cup icing sugar, 1 $^1/_2$ tsp lemon juice

IN large bowl mix together flour, sugar, baking powder, salt, cinnamon and allspice. In separate bowl mix together milk, butter, egg, vanilla, orange rind and lemon rind. Make a well in centre of dry ingredients and add milk mixture. Stir to just combine, then fold in currants. Spoon batter into prepared muffin pans and bake at 190°C for 15–20 minutes. Drizzle a cross on the top with glaze made from icing sugar and lemon juice before serving.

Irish Coffee Muffins

2 cups flour
1 tsp baking powder
$^1/_2$ tsp salt
$^1/_2$ cup sugar
1 egg, beaten
$^1/_3$ cup butter, melted
$^1/_2$ cup heavy cream, unwhipped
$^1/_4$ cup Irish whiskey
$^1/_4$ cup coffee liqueur

PREHEAT oven to 200°C. Sift first 4 ingredients together. Stir in remaining ingredients, until moistened. Three-quarters fill prepared muffin pans, and bake for approximately 20 minutes.

Jaffa Muffins

2 medium-sized oranges
125g butter, softened
1 cup sugar
2 eggs
$^1/_2$ cup natural yoghurt
$^1/_2$ cup orange juice
1 tsp baking powder
$^1/_2$ tsp baking soda
2 cups flour
90g dark chocolate chips

FINELY grate rind of oranges. In large bowl cream butter and sugar until light and fluffy. Beat in eggs and add orange rind. Add yoghurt, orange juice, baking powder and baking soda and stir to combine. Fold in flour and chocolate chips. Spoon batter into prepared muffin pans and bake at 190°C for 15–20 minutes. If desired, ice with chocolate icing and sprinkle with more chocolate chips.

Jam-Filled Muffins

1 1/2 cups flour
1/4 cup sugar
2 tsp baking powder
1/2 tsp baking soda
1/2 tsp salt
1/4 cup butter
1 cup plain yoghurt
1/4 cup milk
1 egg
1/2 tsp vanilla essence
jam or jelly

MIX all dry ingredients. Melt butter. Take off heat and stir in yoghurt and milk; mix. Beat in egg and vanilla. Add butter mixture to dry ingredients and stir until moistened. Spoon half the batter into well-greased muffin pans. Place about 1 tsp jam or jelly into each muffin and then top with remaining batter. Bake at 180°C for 15–20 minutes. Dust with icing sugar.

Jam Surprise Muffins

1 egg
$^3/_4$ cup water
3 tblsp golden syrup
2 cups self-raising flour
$^1/_3$ cup sugar
2 tblsp jam

GENTLY combine all ingredients except jam. One-third fill well-greased muffin pans with mixture. Place a teaspoon of jam in the middle of each muffin and top with remaining mixture. Bake at 200°C for 15 minutes. Take care not to serve muffins before jam centre has cooled.

Kiwifruit Muffins

50g butter
³/₄ cup milk
2 eggs, beaten
1 cup chopped kiwifruit
2 cups flour
2 tsp baking powder
¹/₂ cup brown sugar

M ELT butter and mix with milk and eggs. Add to remaining ingredients and mix until just combined. Spoon into well-greased muffin pans and bake at 200°C for 20–25 minutes.

Kumara & Walnut Muffins

$^3/_4$ cup milk
2 large eggs
$^1/_4$ cup clear honey
2 tblsp oil
1 cup mashed, cooked kumara
2 cups wholemeal flour
2 tsp baking powder
$^1/_2$ tsp salt
1 tsp ground cinnamon
$^1/_2$ cup chopped walnuts

BEAT milk, eggs, honey and oil in large bowl. Stir in kumara. Sift flour, baking powder, salt and cinnamon and stir into kumara mixture. Add walnuts. Divide mixture into prepared muffin pans. Bake at 200°C for 20 minutes or until skewer comes out clean.

Lemon Coconut Muffins

1 cup All-bran
1 1/2 cups Trim milk
1 egg, lightly beaten
2 tblsp oil
grated rind and juice of 1 lemon
1 1/2 cups self-raising flour
1/4 cup caster sugar
1/2 cup coconut
extra coconut for topping

PLACE All-bran and milk in large bowl and let stand for five minutes until softened. Stir in lightly beaten egg, oil, lemon rind and juice. Combine flour, sugar and coconut and stir into All-bran mixture. Mix carefully to just combine. Three-quarters fill greased muffin pans and sprinkle with extra coconut. Bake at 190°C for 25–30 minutes.

Lemon Poppy Seed Muffins

150g butter
3/4 cup sugar
1 egg, beaten
rind and juice of 2 lemons
125g sour cream
1 1/2 cups flour
1 tsp baking powder
1 tsp baking soda
3 tblsp poppy seeds

CREAM butter and sugar, then stir in remaining ingredients until just combined. Spoon into muffin pans lined with paper cases and bake at 160°C for 15–20 minutes. When cool, ice with icing made from the rind and juice of one lemon and sufficient icing sugar to make a smooth paste.

Lemon Sultana Muffins

1 cup sultanas
2 tblsp honey
rind and juice of 2 lemons
$^1/_4$ cup milk
1 cup natural yoghurt
50g butter, melted
1 egg
2 cups flour
2 tsp baking powder
$^1/_3$ cup sugar

BRING sultanas, honey and lemon rind and juice to the boil, then allow to cool. Add remaining ingredients and mix until just combined. Spoon into well-greased muffin pans and bake at 190°C for 12–15 minutes.

Lemon Tea Muffins

1 cup flour
$^1/_2$ cup sugar
1 tsp baking powder
1 tsp salt
$^1/_2$ cup fresh lemon juice
2 eggs
finely grated rind of 1 lemon
60g butter, melted and cooled slightly
Topping
$^1/_4$ cup melted butter
1 tblsp lemon juice
$^1/_2$ cup sugar

IN large bowl mix together flour, sugar, baking powder and salt. In separate bowl add lemon juice, eggs and lemon rind to melted butter. Stir into dry ingredients. Spoon batter into prepared muffin pans and bake at 190°C for 15–20 minutes. Remove from pans while still warm and brush with melted butter and lemon juice mixed together, then sprinkle with sugar.

Little Corn Muffins with Sun-Dried Tomatoes

60g coarse cornmeal
70g plain flour
2 tsp caster sugar
1 ¹/₂ tsp baking powder
¹/₄ tsp salt
1 small egg
100ml milk
1 tblsp corn oil
25g sun-dried tomatoes in oil, drained and finely chopped

STIR all dry ingredients in a bowl. Beat egg with milk and oil and gently mix into flour. Fold chopped sun-dried tomatoes into batter. Spoon into greased muffin pans. Bake at 220°C for 12 minutes. By using coarse-ground cornmeal or polenta, the muffins have a lovely crunchy texture. You could vary the flavour by adding chopped chilli, olives, garlic, etc, to the muffin mix in place of sun-dried tomatoes.

Low-Fat Fruit Muffins

1 egg
1 1/2 tblsp oil
3/4 cup golden syrup
1 3/4 cups flour
2 tsp baking powder
2 tsp baking soda
3/4 cup bran
1 cup unsweetened stewed apple or other fruit
2 cups berries (blueberries, raspberries, blackberries)

MIX all ingredients together until just combined. Spoon into well-greased muffin pans and bake for 25 minutes at 200°C. **Hint**: Replace stewed fruit with canned pie apple or pie fruit, e.g. apple and rhubarb.

Macadamia & White Chocolate Muffins

50g butter, softened
$1/2$ cup caster sugar
1 egg
1 cup milk
2 cups flour
2 tsp baking powder
160g white chocolate, chopped
1 cup chopped macadamia nuts

CREAM butter and sugar until fluffy. Stir in eggs and milk. Mix in flour, baking powder, chocolate and nuts until just combined. Three-quarters fill well-greased muffin pans and bake at 190°C for 20 minutes.

Maggie's Garden Muffins

1 1/2 cups flour
1 cup wholemeal flour
4 tsp baking powder
1/2 tsp salt
1 large egg
2 large egg whites
2/3 cup Trim milk
1/3 cup virgin olive oil
1 cup grated zucchini
3 tblsp minced fresh basil
1 tsp minced garlic
1/3 cup freshly grated Romano cheese
1/2 cup pine nuts

SIFT flours, baking powder and salt into large bowl. In small bowl, whisk together egg, egg whites, milk and oil until well blended. Add egg mixture to dry ingredients and mix gently. Stir in zucchini, basil, garlic, cheese and pine nuts and mix until just combined. Three-quarters fill greased muffin pans and bake at 220°C for about 20 minutes.

Maple Nut Muffins

1 cup wholemeal flour
1 cup flour
2 $^1/_2$ tsp baking powder
$^1/_4$ tsp baking soda
$^1/_2$ tsp salt
$^1/_2$ cup sugar
$^1/_2$ cup chopped nuts
1 egg
$^1/_2$ cup milk
$^1/_4$ cup maple syrup
$^1/_4$ cup oil
$^1/_2$ cup sour cream

IN large bowl mix together flours, baking powder, baking soda, salt, sugar and nuts. In separate bowl mix together egg, milk, maple syrup, oil and sour cream. Add milk mixture to dry ingredients and stir until just moistened. Spoon batter into prepared muffin pans and bake at 200°C for 20 minutes.

Marbled Muffins

$^1/_4$ cup milk
1 egg
50g butter, melted
1 cup natural yoghurt
1 tsp vanilla essence
2 cups flour
2 tsp baking powder
$^1/_3$ cup sugar
1 tsp red food colouring
2 tblsp cocoa mixed with 2 tblsp milk
50g chocolate, grated (optional)

MIX milk, egg, butter, yoghurt and vanilla together. Add flour, baking powder and sugar and mix until just combined. Put 1 tablespoon of mixture into well-greased muffin pans. Divide remaining mixture between two bowls. To one bowl add food colouring, to the other add cocoa mixture and grated chocolate. Put spoonfuls of each mixture into muffin pans and give a quick swirl with a knife. Bake at 190°C for 15–20 minutes.

Mexican Muffins

2 eggs, beaten
³/₄ cup water
1 cup refried beans
1 cup flour
1 tsp salt
1 tblsp baking powder
1 cup grated cheese
2 spring onions, chopped
3 tomatoes, chopped
grated cheese for sprinkling

MIX all ingredients together until just combined. Spoon into well-greased muffin pans and sprinkle with extra grated cheese. Bake at 200°C for 15–20 minutes.

Morning Glory Muffins

4 cups flour
2 $^1/_2$ cups sugar
4 tsp baking soda
4 tsp ground cinnamon
1 tsp salt
2 cups oil
6 eggs, lightly beaten
4 tsp vanilla essence
4 cups grated, peeled apple
1 cup raisins
1 cup flaked coconut
1 cup shredded carrot
1 cup chopped walnuts

IN large bowl combine flour, sugar, baking soda, cinnamon and salt. In separate bowl mix oil, eggs and vanilla. Stir into dry ingredients until just moistened. Fold in apple, raisins, coconut, carrot and nuts. Fill prepared muffin pans two-thirds full. Bake in a 180°C oven for 25–30 minutes. Quantities can be halved.

Moro Bar No-Bake Muffins

3 Moro bars
85g butter
3 1/2 cups rice bubbles
100g dark chocolate, melted

MELT Moro bars and butter together in microwave or over gentle heat on stove, then add rice bubbles and mix well. Mould into muffin shapes in muffin pans lined with paper cases and refrigerate until set. When set, ice with melted chocolate. Store in refrigerator.

Muesli Muffins

1 1/2 cups self-raising flour
100g butter
1 1/2 cups muesli
1 apple, peeled, cored and grated
1/2 cup brown sugar
1/4 cup chopped nuts (optional)
1/2 cup milk
1/2 cup water

SIFT flour and rub in butter until mixture resembles breadcrumbs. Add remaining ingredients and mix until just combined. Three-quarters fill well-greased muffin pans and bake at 190°C for 20–25 minutes.

Mussel, Carrot & Orange Muffins

1 egg
$^1/_2$ cup orange juice
$^1/_2$ cup oil
2 cups flour
$^1/_2$ tsp salt
1 tsp baking powder
1 tsp baking soda
$^1/_2$ cup silverbeet, finely chopped
2 cups grated carrot
grated rind of 1 orange
1 cup cooked mussels, chopped

MAKE egg up to $^1/_2$ cup with water, then add to remaining ingredients and mix until just combined. Three-quarters fill well-greased muffin pans and bake at 200°C for 15–20 minutes.

Oat & Orange Muffins

1 orange, peeled and quartered
2 cups oat bran
¹/₄ cup raw sugar
1 tsp mixed spice
2 tsp baking powder
³/₄ cup sultanas
¹/₄ cup wheatgerm
2 tblsp oil
³/₄ cup milk
1 tsp baking soda
¹/₄ cup chopped walnuts for topping

REMOVE pips and place orange in food processor. Process until finely chopped. In mixing bowl, combine oat bran, sugar, mixed spice, baking powder, sultanas and wheatgerm. Heat oil and milk slightly and dissolve baking soda in milk mixture. Add oat bran mixture and milk to orange in the food processor. Pulse to just combine. Three-quarters fill greased muffin pans, sprinkle with walnuts and bake at 190°C for 15 minutes or until firm.

Oaty Apple Walnut Muffins

100g butter
2 tsp grated lemon rind
$^3/_4$ cup brown sugar
1 egg
1 cup self-raising flour
$^1/_2$ tsp cinnamon
$^1/_4$ tsp baking soda
$^1/_4$ tsp salt
$^3/_4$ cup unsweetened stewed apple
1 cup quick-cooking rolled oats
$^1/_2$ cup sultanas
$^1/_2$ cup chopped walnuts

CREAM butter, lemon rind and sugar. Add egg and beat well. Sift flour, cinnamon, baking soda and salt, and add alternately to creamed mixture with stewed apples. Fold in oats, sultanas and walnuts. Three-quarters fill greased muffin pans and bake at 180°C for 20–25 minutes.

Olive Muffins

1 cup (300g) chopped pitted black olives
2 cups flour
¹/₂ cup grated onion
³/₄ cup olive oil, plus additional oil to brush muffin pans
1 ¹/₂ tblsp chopped fresh mint, or 1 tsp crushed dried mint
1 tblsp sugar
1 heaped tsp baking powder

PREHEAT oven to 190°C. Rinse olives and drain. Dry on paper towels. Combine all ingredients, adding baking powder last. Brush muffin pans with oil and dust with flour. Bake for 20–25 minutes, or until golden.

Olive & Chilli Muffins

1 egg
$^3/_4$ cup water
2 cups flour
$^1/_2$ tsp salt
1 tblsp baking powder
1 $^1/_2$ cups grated cheddar
$^1/_2$ cup pitted black olives, sliced
1 tsp whole dried chilli, very finely sliced
2 tblsp cornmeal

MIX all ingredients except cornmeal until just combined. Spoon into well-greased muffin pans and sprinkle with cornmeal. Bake at 200°C for 12–15 minutes.

Olive & Salami Muffins

1 egg, beaten
1 cup flour
¹/₄ tsp salt
1 tblsp baking powder
¹/₂ cup grated cheese
²/₃ cup pitted black olives, sliced
²/₃ cup cubed spicy salami

MAKE egg up to one cup with water and mix with remaining ingredients until just combined. Three-quarters fill well-greased muffin pans and bake at 200°C for 12–15 minutes.

Orange Muffins

rind and flesh of 2 oranges (pith and seeds discarded)
75g butter, softened
1 egg
1 ¹/₂ cups self-raising flour
³/₄ cup sugar
¹/₂ cup currants

PROCESS orange rind and flesh with butter and egg. Mix in remaining ingredients until just combined. Spoon into well-greased muffin pans and bake at 190°C for 15–20 minutes.

Orange Carrot Muffins

1 1/2 cups wholemeal flour
1/2 cup oat bran
2 tsp baking powder
1/2 tsp baking soda
1 tsp cinnamon
1 egg
2/3 cup orange juice
1/2 cup buttermilk
2 tblsp sugar
1 tsp grated orange peel
2 tblsp oil
1 cup coarsely grated carrot

IN large bowl, mix together flour, oat bran, baking powder, baking soda and cinnamon. In separate bowl, beat together egg, juice, buttermilk, sugar, orange peel and oil. Mixture will look curdled, but don't worry. Stir in carrot. Add wet ingredients to dry ingredients, and stir until just moistened. Divide batter between muffin pans. Bake for approximately 20 minutes in a 200°C oven.

Orange Chocolate Chip Muffins

2 cups flour
$^1/_2$ cup brown sugar, firmly packed
$^1/_2$ cup sugar
1 $^1/_2$ tsp baking powder
$^1/_2$ tsp baking soda
$^1/_2$ tsp salt
$^1/_3$ cup oil
$^1/_4$ cup orange juice
$^1/_4$ cup orange liqueur
1 egg
1 tsp grated orange rind
1 tsp vanilla essence
1 cup chocolate chips
icing sugar or cocoa for dusting

IN large bowl mix together flour, sugars, baking powder, baking soda and salt. In separate bowl mix together oil, orange juice, liqueur, egg, orange rind and vanilla. Make well in centre of dry ingredients and add orange mixture. Stir to combine, then fold in chocolate chips. Spoon batter into prepared muffin pans and bake at 200°C for 15–20 minutes. Serve dusted with icing sugar or cocoa. **Variation**: Top with orange icing and sprinkle with chocolate chips.

Orange Marmalade Muffins

1 1/2 cups self-raising flour
1 1/4 cups All-bran
1/2 cup chopped walnuts
1 egg
grated rind and juice of 1 orange
1/2 cup marmalade
1/4 cup Trim milk
1/4 cup oil
Sugar 'n' Spice Topping
2 tblsp brown sugar, 2 tblsp caster sugar, 1/4 tsp cinnamon, ground nutmeg
to taste, 1/4 cup plain flour, shredded orange rind, 1 1/2 tblsp butter

COMBINE flour, All-bran and walnuts in large bowl. Beat egg, orange rind and juice, marmalade, milk and oil. Add to dry ingredients and mix until just combined. For topping, combine all dry ingredients and orange rind. Rub in butter until mixture resembles breadcrumbs. Three-quarters fill greased muffin pans and sprinkle each muffin with a little of the topping. Bake at 200°C for 20 minutes.

Orange Toasted Almond Muffins

2 ¹/₂ cups flour
1 cup sugar
3 ¹/₂ tsp baking powder
¹/₂ tsp salt
¹/₄ tsp almond essence
1 tblsp grated orange rind
¹/₃ cup oil
³/₄ cup evaporated milk
¹/₂ cup water
1 egg
1 cup toasted finely chopped almonds
1 cup sifted icing sugar
1–2 tblsp orange juice

IN large bowl combine flour, sugar, baking powder, salt, almond essence, orange rind, oil, evaporated milk, water and egg; beat with electric mixer at high speed for 30 seconds until blended. Fold in ³/₄ cup chopped almonds. Spoon batter into prepared muffin pans to two-thirds full. Bake at 190°C for 15–18 minutes. In small bowl combine icing sugar and orange juice. Spread over muffins. Sprinkle with remaining almonds.

Overnight Bran Muffins

1 egg
1 ½ cups natural yoghurt
½ cup oil
1 ½ cups flour
1 tsp baking soda
1 tsp ground cinnamon
1 ½ cups bran
½ cup brown sugar
125g dates, chopped

MIX all ingredients together until just combined. Cover mixture and leave in fridge for up to 24 hours. Spoon into well-greased muffin pans and bake at 180°C for 15–20 minutes.

Passionfruit Crunch Muffins

1 egg
$^1/_2$ cup milk
$^1/_3$ cup honey
$^1/_3$ cup oil
2 cups flour
1 tsp baking powder
$^1/_2$ cup passionfruit pulp
Topping
50g butter
$^1/_2$ cup brown sugar
$^1/_2$ cup rolled oats

MIX all muffin ingredients together until just combined. Three-quarters fill well-greased muffin pans and sprinkle with topping made by rubbing butter and sugar together and mixing in rolled oats. Bake at 180°C for 15–20 minutes.

Passover Ginger Muffins

³/₄ cup potato flour or rice flour
¹/₂ tsp ground cinnamon
¹/₂ tsp ground ginger
¹/₈ tsp ground cloves
1 whole egg
2 tblsp honey
2 tsp freshly grated orange peel
2 tblsp freshly squeezed orange juice
4 egg whites
2 tblsp sugar

IN large bowl, mix together potato flour and spices. In small bowl, whisk together whole egg, honey, orange peel and juice. Add to dry ingredients, and stir together until just blended. Batter will be stiff. In deep, medium-sized bowl, beat egg whites until soft peaks form. Add sugar, and beat until whites are thick and glossy. Stir about ¹/₄ of egg white mixture into potato flour batter, and then fold in remaining egg whites. Spoon batter into muffin pans and bake at 200°C for about 15 minutes. Let cool for about 10 minutes before removing from pans. Best served warm.

Peach Muffins

2 cups canned or fresh peaches, drained
4 cups flour
2 cups sugar
2 tsp baking powder
$1/2$ tsp salt
3 eggs
$3/4$ cup oil
2 cups milk
Topping
$1/2$ cup sugar
1 tsp cinnamon

DICE drained peaches to the size of peas. Mix flour, sugar, baking powder and salt. Set aside. In separate bowl combine eggs and oil, and fold in milk. Add flour mixture and combine gently. Fold in peaches. Spoon into prepared muffin pans, sprinkle with topping and bake in preheated oven at 200°C for 20–25 minutes.

Peanut Butter Muffins

1 1/2 cups flour
2 tsp baking powder
1/2 cup sugar
1/2 tsp salt
60g butter
1/2 cup crunchy peanut butter
2 eggs, beaten
1 cup milk

IN large bowl mix together flour, baking powder, sugar and salt.
Cut in butter and peanut butter and mix until crumbly. Add
eggs and milk and stir until just combined. Spoon batter into
prepared muffin pans and bake at 190°C for 15–20 minutes.
Variation: Brush tops of hot muffins with melted jam, then
sprinkle with chopped peanuts.

Pear & Honey Muffins

1 egg
1 cup natural yoghurt
1/4 cup lemon juice
50g butter, melted
1/2 cup honey
2 cups wholemeal flour
1 tsp baking powder
1 tsp baking soda
1/2 cup brown sugar
2 large pears, peeled, cored and diced
honey for pouring

MIX all ingredients together until just combined. Three-quarters fill well-greased muffin pans and bake at 190°C for 15–20 minutes. Pour a little extra honey on top of each muffin while still warm.

Pecan Cinnamon Muffins

1 1/2 cups flour, sifted
1/4 cup sugar
1/4 cup brown sugar, packed
2 tsp baking powder
1/2 tsp salt
1/2 tsp ground cinnamon
1 large egg, lightly beaten
1/2 cup oil
1/2 cup milk
1/2 cup chopped pecans

SIFT together flour, sugar, brown sugar, baking powder, salt and cinnamon into mixing bowl. Combine egg, oil and milk in small bowl; blend well. Add to dry ingredients, stirring just enough to moisten. Fold in pecans. Spoon batter into greased muffin pans, filling each two-thirds full. Bake in 200°C oven for 20 minutes or until golden brown.

Pecan Pumpkin Muffins

$^1/_2$ cup water
$^1/_2$ cup milk
1 $^1/_2$ cups pumpkin, cooked and mashed
50g butter, melted
2 cups wholemeal flour
2 tsp baking powder
1 tsp ground nutmeg
$^1/_4$ cup brown sugar
$^1/_2$ cup pecan halves

STIR water and milk into pumpkin, add remaining ingredients and mix until just combined. Three-quarters fill well-greased muffin pans with mixture and bake at 220°C for 15–20 minutes.

Persimmon Muffins

1 cup wholemeal flour
1 cup flour
1 tsp baking powder
$^1/_2$ tsp salt
$^1/_2$ tsp ground cinnamon
$^1/_2$ tsp ground nutmeg
$^1/_4$ tsp ground cloves
$^1/_2$ cup mashed persimmon pulp
$^1/_2$ cup raisins
1 egg
$^1/_2$ cup milk
$^1/_3$ cup oil
$^1/_2$ cup honey
Icing
1 $^1/_2$ cups icing sugar, $^1/_2$ tsp vanilla essence, 2 tblsp brandy

MIX together flours, baking powder, salt and spices. In separate bowl mix together remaining ingredients. Add liquid ingredients to dry ingredients and combine until just moistened. Spoon batter into prepared muffin pans and bake at 200°C for 18 minutes. Allow to cool before icing. To make icing, mix ingredients together thoroughly.

Pineapple Muffins

2 cups flour
1 tsp baking powder
1 cup sugar
1 tsp salt
1 egg
1 cup milk
1 tblsp butter, melted
1/2 cup drained, crushed pineapple

SIFT dry ingredients. Beat egg with milk, and add butter and pineapple. Make a well in centre of dry ingredients, add liquid and stir until just damp and lumpy. Three-quarters fill greased muffin pans and bake at 200°C for 15–20 minutes.

Pineapple-Ricotta Muffins

1 egg, lightly beaten
oil
1 1/2 cups ricotta cheese
1 cup crushed pineapple
2 cups flour
1/2 cup sugar
1 tblsp baking powder
1/2 tsp baking soda
1/2 tsp salt

PLACE egg in a measuring cup and add enough oil to make half a cup. In large mixing bowl, add egg and oil to ricotta cheese and mix well. Stir in crushed pineapple. In separate bowl, combine dry ingredients, then add to wet ingredients and blend gently, until flour mixture is just absorbed. Fill greased muffin pans two-thirds full. Bake at 200ºC for about 25 minutes.

Pine Nut & Yoghurt Muffins

2 cups flour
$^1/_4$ cup sugar
1 tsp baking soda
$^1/_4$ tsp salt
1 cup natural yoghurt
$^1/_4$ cup milk
60g butter, melted and cooled slightly
1 egg
2 tblsp honey
1 tsp vanilla essence
$^3/_4$ cup chopped dried apricots
$^1/_2$ cup chopped pine nuts

IN large bowl stir together flour, sugar, baking soda and salt. In separate bowl mix together yoghurt, milk, butter, egg, honey and vanilla until well combined. Make a well in centre of dry ingredients and add yoghurt mixture. Stir to just combine. Mix in apricots and all but 2 tablespoons of pine nuts. Spoon batter into prepared muffin pans and sprinkle with reserved pine nuts. Bake at 200°C for 15–20 minutes.

Pistachio Muffins

1 egg
¹/₂ cup water
50g butter, melted
1 cup natural yoghurt
2 cups flour
¹/₄ tsp salt
2 tsp baking powder
¹/₄ cup sugar
1 cup chopped pistachio nuts

MIX all ingredients together until just combined. Spoon into well-greased muffin pans and bake at 190°C for 15–20 minutes.

Pistachio Chocolate Muffins

$^1/_3$ cup butter
2 cups flour
3 tsp baking powder
1 tsp salt
$^1/_3$ cup sugar
2 eggs
1 cup milk
2 tsp rum
$^1/_2$ cup chopped pistachio nuts
$^1/_2$ cup chocolate bits
$^1/_3$ cup finely chopped pistachio nuts

RUB butter into flour, baking powder and salt. Add sugar. Beat eggs, milk and rum. Make a well in centre of dry ingredients and add milk mixture, chopped nuts and chocolate bits. Mix very lightly until just combined. Three-quarters fill greased muffin pans and sprinkle with finely chopped pistachio nuts. Bake at 200°C for 20–25 minutes.

Pizza Muffins

2 cups flour
$^1/_2$ tsp salt
1 tblsp baking powder
1 onion, chopped
1 cup grated cheese
1 rasher bacon, cooked and chopped
1 tomato, chopped
1 egg, lightly beaten

MIX first seven ingredients together. Make egg up to 1 cup with water, then mix with dry ingredients until just combined. Spoon into well-greased muffin pans and bake at 200°C for 20 minutes.

Plantation Muffins

1 cup chopped pecans
2 cups flour
1 tsp baking soda
1 tsp salt
90g softened cream cheese
1 cup sugar
2 tsp vanilla
1 beaten egg
$^1/_2$ cup sour cream
550g crushed pineapple

HEAVILY grease muffin pans and sprinkle with chopped pecans. Set aside. Sift together flour, baking soda and salt and set aside. In separate bowl, beat cream cheese, sugar and vanilla, then add beaten egg. Mix in flour mixture alternately with sour cream until just combined. Fold in drained pineapple. Bake in a 200°C oven for 20–25 minutes.

Plum Muffins

10 to 12 dark ripe plums
3 cups flour
1 tblsp baking powder
$^3/_4$ cup sugar
1 tblsp grated lemon rind
50g butter, melted
2 eggs, lightly beaten
1 $^1/_4$ cups milk
extra 2 tblsp sugar

PEEL and stone plums, and roughly chop flesh. Set aside. Sift flour and baking powder and stir in first measure of sugar and lemon rind. Combine melted butter and lightly beaten eggs, and add milk. Pour milk mixture into flour. Gently stir to just mix. Fold in chopped plums. Three-quarters fill greased muffin pans. Sprinkle with extra sugar. Bake at 200°C for 15–20 minutes.

Potato Fry Muffins

2 potatoes, peeled and cubed
1 clove garlic, crushed
1 tsp mustard seeds
1 tsp turmeric
1 tblsp oil
1 egg, lightly beaten
1 cup flour
1 tblsp baking powder
1 tsp salt
1 cup grated cheese

FRY potato with garlic, mustard seeds, turmeric and oil until potato is tender but not soft. Beware – the mustard seeds may jump around. Transfer to a bowl. Make egg up to 1 cup with water. Add egg and remaining ingredients to potato mixture and stir until just combined. Spoon into well-greased muffin pans and bake at 180°C for 12–15 minutes.

Potato & Sun-Dried Tomato Muffins

3 cups peeled and grated potatoes
1 clove garlic, finely chopped
8 sun-dried tomatoes, finely chopped
$^1/_2$ cup flour
$^1/_2$ tsp salt
1 tsp baking powder
3 tblsp olive oil
2 egg yolks
2 egg whites, beaten to a soft snow

RINSE and drain potatoes. Mix with all ingredients except egg whites. Fold in egg whites. Spoon into greased muffin pans. Bake at 200°C for 20–25 minutes.

Pumpkin Muffins

2 tblsp butter
$^1/_2$ cup sugar
1 egg
$^3/_4$ cup flour
1 tsp baking powder
1 tsp baking soda
$^1/_2$ tsp ground cinnamon
$^1/_4$ tsp ground nutmeg
$^3/_4$ cup wholemeal flour
$^1/_4$ cup sultanas
$^1/_2$ cup mashed cooked pumpkin
milk to mix

CREAM butter and sugar, then add egg and beat. Sift flour, baking powder, baking soda and spices into creamed mixture. Stir in wholemeal flour, sultanas, pumpkin and sufficient milk to make a moist mixture. Spoon batter into prepared muffin pans and bake at 180°C for 15–20 minutes. If desired, ice with cream cheese and icing sugar mixed together.

Pumpkin & Chocolate Chip Muffins

1 cup sliced almonds
1 3/4 cups flour
1 tsp allspice
1 tsp garam masala
1/4 tsp baking powder
1 tsp baking soda
1/4 tsp salt
1 cup sugar
2 eggs
1 cup cooked mashed pumpkin
150g butter, melted
1 cup chocolate chips

PLACE almonds on oven tray and bake at 180°C for about five minutes or until lightly browned. Sift flour, allspice, garam masala, baking powder, baking soda and salt. Add sugar. In separate bowl, beat eggs and add pumpkin and melted butter. Beat to combine. Fold almonds and chocolate chips into this mixture. Quickly fold in dry ingredients. Three-quarters fill greased muffin pans and bake at 180°C for 20 minutes or until well risen.

Raisin Muffins

1 1/2 cups wholemeal flour
1/3 cup brown sugar
3 tsp baking powder
1/2 tsp salt
1 tsp cinnamon
1/2 cup wheatgerm
3/4 cup raisins
2/3 cup milk
1/3 cup oil
2 eggs, lightly beaten

SIFT flour, adding any husks in sifter to the bowl. Mix in sugar, baking powder, salt, cinnamon, wheatgerm and raisins. Add milk, oil and lightly beaten eggs. Mix until dry ingredients are just moistened. Three-quarters fill greased muffin pans and bake at 200°C for 20 minutes.

Rhubarb Muffins

2 cups flour
4 tsp baking powder
¹/₂ tsp salt
³/₄ cup sugar
1 cup milk
100g butter, melted and cooled slightly
1 egg
1 ¹/₂ cups finely chopped rhubarb
3 tblsp raw sugar for sprinkling
1 tblsp ground cinnamon for sprinkling

SIFT together flour, baking powder and salt. Add sugar and combine. In separate bowl mix together milk, butter and egg. Add milk mixture to dry ingredients and combine, then stir in rhubarb. Spoon batter into prepared muffin pans. Mix together raw sugar and cinnamon and sprinkle over. Bake at 220°C for 15 minutes. Delicious served with whipped cream.

Rice Muffins

1 egg
1 cup milk
1 tblsp golden syrup
1 cup cooked rice
2 cups flour
2 tsp baking powder
$1/4$ tsp nutmeg
$1/2$ cup sultanas

MIX all ingredients until just combined. Spoon into well-greased muffin pans and bake at 180°C for 15 minutes.

Rocky Road Muffins

$1/4$ cup milk
1 egg
1 cup natural yoghurt
50g butter, melted
2 cups flour
1 tsp baking powder
$1/2$ cup sugar
$1/2$ cup small marshmallows
$1/2$ cup roughly chopped chocolate
$1/2$ cup peanuts
$1/2$ cup jubes

MIX milk, egg, yoghurt and butter. Add remaining ingredients and mix until just combined. Spoon into well-greased muffin pans and bake at 180°C for 12–15 minutes.

Hint: Top with icing made from 1 tblsp each cocoa, butter and milk heated together and mixed with sufficient icing sugar to make a paste. Set marshmallows or jubes in icing before it sets.

Salmon Muffins

1 x 185g can salmon, drained and mashed (reserve liquid)
1 egg
1 cup flour
1 tsp salt
1 tblsp baking powder
1 cup grated mild cheese

MAKE liquid from salmon up to ³/₄ cup with water and mix into remaining ingredients until just combined. Three-quarters fill well-greased muffin pans and bake at 200°C for 12–15 minutes. **Hint**: Make a small diagonal split in the top of each muffin before serving, spread with cream cheese and tuck in a small piece of smoked salmon.

Savoury Cottage Cheese Muffins

2 cups flour
$^1/_2$ tsp salt
1 tsp dry mustard
2 $^1/_2$ tsp baking powder
25g butter
1 egg
$^3/_4$ cup milk
250g cottage cheese
$^1/_4$ cup chopped parsley
1 small onion, finely chopped
$^1/_4$ cup grated tasty cheese
$^1/_4$ tsp paprika

SIFT flour, salt, mustard and baking powder. Rub in butter. Beat together egg and milk, then add cottage cheese, parsley and onion. Mix well. Stir liquid into dry ingredients until just combined. Three-quarters fill greased muffin pans, then sprinkle mixed grated cheese and paprika over muffins. Bake at 200°C for 20 minutes. Serve warm.

Self-Saucing Chocolate Muffins

¹/₂ cup white sugar
1 cup self-raising flour
1 tblsp cocoa
¹/₂ cup milk
1 tblsp butter, melted
1 tblsp cocoa
1 cup brown sugar
1 ¹/₂ cups boiling water

MIX white sugar, flour and first measure of cocoa in a bowl. Add milk and melted butter, stir until just combined and half fill well-greased muffin pans with mixture. Mix second measure of cocoa with brown sugar and boiling water, and add to each muffin pan to take level up to three-quarters full. Bake at 180°C for 15–20 minutes. To turn muffins out, place serving dish over muffin pans and carefully flip over. Scoop out any remaining sauce.

Skagit Berry Oatmeal Muffins

$^1/_2$ cup oatmeal
$^1/_2$ cup oat bran
1 $^1/_2$ cups flour
$^1/_2$ cup sugar
1 tsp salt
1 tblsp baking powder
1 egg
$^3/_4$ cup milk
$^1/_2$ cup vegetable oil
1 cup mixed berries (blueberries, raspberries, strawberries or blackberries)
Topping
$^1/_3$ cup oatmeal
$^1/_4$ cup brown sugar
1 tsp cinnamon

COMBINE dry ingredients in large bowl. In separate bowl mix together egg, milk and oil. Mix wet ingredients into flour mixture. Gently stir in mixed berries until just mixed and lumpy. Spoon batter into greased muffin pans. Sprinkle batter with topping. Bake at 200°C for about 20 minutes.

Sliced Banana Muffins

1 ½ cups flour
⅓ cup sugar
50g butter
1 tsp baking powder
2 bananas, thinly sliced
1 egg
½ cup milk
100g chocolate, chopped

RUB flour, sugar and butter together until mixture resembles breadcrumbs. Add remaining ingredients and mix until just combined. Spoon into well-greased muffin pans and bake at 190°C for 20 minutes.

Sour Cream Jalapeno Corn Muffins

1 1/2 cups yellow cornmeal
1/2 cup flour
1 tblsp granulated sugar
1 tblsp baking powder
1 tsp salt
2 large eggs
1 cup sour cream
1–1 1/2 tsp minced and seeded jalapeno pepper

THOROUGHLY mix cornmeal, flour, sugar, baking powder and salt in large bowl. Beat eggs and sour cream with a whisk or fork in a small bowl. When smooth, stir in jalapeno pepper. Pour over flour mixture. Fold in with a rubber spatula until well mixed; batter will be very stiff. Scoop batter into well-greased muffin pans. Bake at 180ºC for 20–25 minutes, or until firm to the touch in the centre. Let cool 5 minutes in pans before turning out onto a cooling rack.

Spiced Apple Muffins

2 eggs
1 cup water
2 cups wholemeal flour
$^1/_4$ tsp salt
1 tblsp baking powder
1 tsp ground cinnamon
1 tsp mixed spice
$^1/_2$ cup brown sugar
2 cups cooked apple cubes (or canned pie apple)
coffee sugar

MIX together all ingredients except coffee sugar until just combined. Three-quarters fill well-greased muffin pans and sprinkle with coffee sugar. Bake at 190°C for 20-25 minutes.

Spiced Lemon Muffins

2 cups flour
1 ¹/₂ tsp ground cinnamon
4 tsp baking powder
1 tblsp grated lemon rind
¹/₂ cup sugar
2 eggs
¹/₂ cup oil
1 cup natural yoghurt
¹/₄ cup milk
¹/₄ cup raw sugar for sprinkling
1 tsp ground cinnamon for sprinkling
Topping
2 eggs, ¹/₂ cup sugar, grated rind & juice of 2 lemons, 2 tblsp butter

IN large bowl mix flour, cinnamon, baking powder, lemon rind and sugar. In separate bowl beat eggs, oil, yoghurt and milk. Add yoghurt mixture to dry ingredients, stir to combine. Spoon into prepared muffin pans and sprinkle with raw sugar and cinnamon mixed together. Bake at 200°C for 15-20 minutes. To make topping, combine eggs and sugar in heatproof bowl. Stir in lemon rind, lemon juice and butter. Cook in bowl over saucepan of boiling water for 15 minutes, stirring occasionally, until mixture thickens. Spread on cooled muffins.

Spicy All-Bran Muffins

1 1/4 cups All-bran
1 1/2 cups Trim milk
1 egg yolk
60g butter, melted
1/2 cup chopped raisins or dates
1 1/2 cups self-raising flour
1 tsp cinnamon
1/2 tsp nutmeg
1/4 cup caster sugar
2 egg whites, stiffly beaten
extra All-bran for topping

PLACE All-bran and milk in large bowl and let stand for five minutes until softened. Beat in egg yolk, melted butter and raisins. Sift flour and spices. Stir in sugar and add to All-bran mixture. Fold in stiffly beaten egg whites. Three-quarters fill greased muffin pans and sprinkle with extra All-bran. Bake at 200°C for 25–30 minutes.

Spicy Fruit Muffins

50g butter
1/2 cup sugar
1 egg
1 grated apple
1/2 tsp baking soda
1 dessertspoon boiling water
3/4 cup flour
1/2 tsp cinnamon
1/2 tsp mixed spice
1/4 cup sultanas

CREAM butter and sugar. Add egg and beat well. Stir in grated apple, soda dissolved in water, flour and spices. Mix lightly, then fold in sultanas. Three-quarters fill greased muffin pans and bake at 200°C for 15 minutes or until firm.

Spicy Nut Muffins

1 tblsp olive oil
1 cup nuts (almonds, peanuts, cashews, walnuts)
1 garlic clove, crushed
1 tsp salt
$^1/_4$ tsp each ground cumin, coriander, chilli powder, ginger and cinnamon
1 egg, beaten
$^1/_4$ cup water
1 cup natural yoghurt
50g butter, melted
2 tblsp honey
2 cups self-raising flour

HEAT oil in frying pan and gently fry nuts, garlic, salt and spices for 15 minutes. Leave to cool. Mix remaining ingredients together until just combined. Add nuts, reserving quarter of a cup for decoration. Three-quarters fill well-greased muffin pans and sprinkle with reserved nuts. Bake at 200°C for 15–20 minutes.

Spicy Prune Muffins

1 tsp baking soda
³/₄ cup warm milk
1 egg
¹/₃ cup oil
2 cups self-raising flour
1 tsp mixed spice
¹/₂ cup brown sugar
³/₄ cup prunes soaked in ¹/₄ cup liqueur

S TIR baking soda into milk. Mix remaining ingredients until just combined, then add milk mixture and stir gently to mix. Spoon into well-greased muffin pans and bake at 190°C for 20–25 minutes.

Spicy Pumpkin Muffins

1 cup plain flour
1 cup wholemeal flour
¹/₄ cup sugar
1 tblsp baking powder
¹/₂ tblsp each ground cinnamon and nutmeg
¹/₂ tsp each ground ginger and cloves
2 eggs
¹/₄ cup oil
³/₄ cup low-fat milk
1 cup pumpkin purée

IN large bowl, mix dry ingredients. In separate bowl, beat together eggs, oil, milk and pumpkin. Add to dry ingredients and stir until just combined. Spoon into prepared muffin pans. Bake at 200°C for 20–25 minutes.

Spinach & Caramelised Onion Muffins

2 onions, diced
1 tsp olive oil
1 bunch spinach, washed and spun dry
2 1/2 cups flour
1/4 cup sugar
1 tsp baking powder
2 tsp salt
2 eggs
3/4 cup milk
2/3 cup oil
1/2 cup grated Parmesan cheese for top

COOK the diced onions slowly over medium-high heat in olive oil until they become richly caramelised. Remove to cool. Add the spinach to the pan and cook over high heat until the leaves become completely wilted. Remove to cool. When cool, chop finely. Reserve. Combine four dry ingredients in bowl and mix. Add eggs, milk and oil to dry ingredients along with cooled onions and spinach. Mix together until just combined. Scoop batter into buttered muffin pans, filling two-thirds full. Sprinkle tops of batter with Parmesan cheese. Bake at 215°C for about 15 minutes.

Spinach & Feta Muffins

1 egg
$^3/_4$ cup water
2 cups self-raising flour
$^1/_2$ tsp salt
1 clove garlic, crushed
100g feta cheese, crumbled
1 cup finely shredded spinach
$^2/_3$ cup grated cheddar
$^1/_4$ cup grated Parmesan cheese

MIX together all ingredients except Parmesan cheese until just combined. Spoon into well-greased muffin pans and sprinkle with Parmesan. Bake at 180°C for 15–20 minutes.

Squashed Grape Muffins

1 egg
³/₄ cup water
2 tblsp honey
2 cups self-raising flour
¹/₃ cup sugar
small bunch grapes
sugar for sprinkling

MIX together egg, water, honey, flour and sugar until just combined. One-third fill well-greased muffin pans with mixture. Place three or four grapes, squashed with the blade of a strong knife, in middle of each muffin and sprinkle with a little sugar. Top with remaining mixture and sprinkle with more sugar. Bake at 200°C for 15 minutes. Take care not to serve muffins before sugar in centre has cooled.

Strawberry Muffins

3 cups flour
$^1/_2$ cup sugar
$^1/_2$ cup brown sugar
1 tblsp baking powder
125g butter, melted and cooled slightly
3 eggs
1 cup milk
1 $^1/_2$ cups chopped strawberries
icing sugar for dusting

IN large bowl mix together flour, sugars and baking powder. In separate bowl mix together butter, eggs and milk. Add to dry ingredients then fold in berries. Brush oil onto bottoms of muffin pans only. Spoon batter into pans and bake at 200°C for 20 minutes. Serve hot, dusted with icing sugar. **Variation**: Allow muffins to cool and serve with fresh whipped cream and strawberries.

Strawberry Rhubarb Muffins

1 cup rolled oats
1 cup strawberry yoghurt
125g butter, melted
$^1/_2$ cup brown sugar
1 egg
1 cup flour
$^1/_2$ tsp salt
1 tsp baking powder
$^1/_2$ tsp baking soda
1 tsp cinnamon
$^3/_4$ cup bran
$^3/_4$ cup finely chopped rhubarb
6 tblsp strawberry jam

SOAK rolled oats in strawberry yoghurt for five minutes. Stir melted butter and brown sugar into yoghurt. Lightly beat egg and add to yoghurt mixture. Sift flour, salt, baking powder, baking soda and cinnamon and add with bran to yoghurt mixture. Stir until dry ingredients are just moistened. Fold in chopped rhubarb and strawberry jam. Three-quarters fill greased muffin pans and bake at 190°C for 15–20 minutes.

Strawberry Yoghurt Muffins

1 3/4 cups wholemeal flour
1/2 cup caster sugar
2 eggs, beaten
60g butter, melted and cooled slightly
2/3 cup milk
1/3 cup strawberry yoghurt
coconut for sprinkling

IN large bowl mix together flour and sugar. In separate bowl mix together eggs, butter and milk. Add milk mixture to dry ingredients and stir until just combined. Spoon batter into prepared muffin pans and bake at 190°C for 15–20 minutes. Allow to cool, then slice off tops and cut each top in half. Drop a teaspoonful of yoghurt onto cut surface of muffin and push straight edges of tops into yoghurt. Sprinkle with coconut.

Sugared Walnut Muffins

1 cup walnut halves
1 egg white, whisked
$^1/_3$ cup caster sugar
1 tsp cinnamon
1 egg
$^3/_4$ cup water
2 cups self-raising flour
$^1/_2$ cup sugar
2 tblsp honey

SOAK walnuts in egg white for five minutes, then drain in a sieve for two minutes. Toss walnuts in caster sugar and cinnamon. Bake at 160°C for 15-20 minutes, being careful not to let them burn. Leave to cool. Mix walnuts with remaining ingredients until just combined. Spoon into well-greased muffin pans and bake at 180°C for 12-15 minutes.

Sultana Bran Muffins

1 1/3 cups flour
1 1/2 tblsp baking powder
1/4 tsp salt
1/2 tsp cinnamon
1 1/3 cups milk
3 cups sultana bran
2 eggs, well beaten
1/4 cup melted butter
1/2 cup honey

SIFT together flour, baking powder, salt and cinnamon. Pour milk over sultana bran, stir, and let stand 5 minutes. Stir in eggs, melted butter and honey. Add dry ingredients and stir just until moistened. Spoon batter into greased muffin pans. Bake at 200°C for 20 minutes.

Sultana & Pineapple Muffins

1 x 450g can crushed pineapple
1 cup sultanas
1 cup sugar
125g butter
1 tsp mixed spice
$^1/_4$ tsp salt
2 eggs
2 cups flour
1 $^1/_2$ tsp baking powder
icing sugar for dusting

TIP crushed pineapple into a saucepan and add sultanas, sugar, butter, mixed spice and salt. Bring to the boil, stirring, until butter melts. Simmer for 5 minutes, then allow to cool slightly. Beat in eggs. Combine flour and baking powder and add to pineapple mixture. Stir to combine. Spoon batter into prepared muffin pans and bake at 180°C for 15–20 minutes. Serve dusted with icing sugar. If desired, fill with whipped cream mixed with drained crushed pineapple.

Sultana Sesame Muffins

2 cups flour
$^1/_4$ cup sugar
4 tsp baking powder
1 tsp salt (optional)
$^1/_2$ tsp ginger
$^1/_4$ tsp cinnamon
$^3/_4$ cup chopped sultanas
1 egg
1 cup milk
$^1/_3$ cup butter, melted
Topping
1 tblsp sesame seeds
1 tblsp brown sugar
pinch of ginger

SIFT flour, sugar, baking powder, salt, first measure of ginger and cinnamon. Add sultanas and mix well. In small bowl, beat egg and add milk and melted butter. Stir into flour mixture until just combined. Three-quarters fill greased muffin pans. Combine sesame seeds, brown sugar and pinch of ginger and sprinkle over muffins. Bake at 220°C for 20–25 minutes.

Sun-Dried Tomato & Herb Muffins

1 egg, beaten
1 cup flour
$^1/_4$ tsp salt
1 tblsp baking powder
2 tblsp chopped fresh herbs
1 $^1/_2$ cups grated cheese
$^1/_2$ cup sun-dried tomatoes in oil, chopped

MAKE egg up to one cup with water and mix with remaining ingredients until just combined. Three-quarters fill well-greased muffin pans and bake at 200°C for 12–15 minutes.

Sweet Sherry Currant Muffins

$^1/_2$ cup currants
2 tblsp sweet sherry
100g butter, softened
$^1/_2$ cup packed brown sugar
2 eggs
2 cups plain flour
3 tsp baking powder
$^1/_2$ tsp baking soda
$^1/_2$ tsp salt
1 $^1/_4$ cups buttermilk (or soured milk)
Topping
2 tblsp caster sugar
1 tsp cinnamon

SOAK currants in sherry until plump. Beat softened butter and brown sugar until fluffy. Beat in eggs then stir in currants. Sift flour, baking powder, baking soda and salt, and fold into creamed mixture alternately with buttermilk. Mix until just combined. Three-quarters fill greased muffin pans. Combine caster sugar and cinnamon and sprinkle over muffins. Bake at 200°C for 15 minutes until browned.

Tamarillo & Spice Muffins

2 cups flour
$^1/_2$ cup sugar
2 $^1/_2$ tsp baking powder
2 tsp mixed spice
1 egg, beaten
$^1/_2$ cup milk
100g butter, melted and cooled slightly
4 tamarillos, peeled and chopped
Filling
whipped cream
sugar
chopped tamarillo

IN large bowl mix together flour, sugar, baking powder and mixed spice. In separate bowl mix together egg, milk and butter. Add milk mixture and tamarillos to dry ingredients and stir to just combine. Spoon batter into prepared muffin pans and bake at 200°C for 20 minutes. Serve filled with sweetened whipped cream into which chopped tamarillo has been folded.

Tapenade & Olive Muffins

1 egg, beaten
1/2 cup tapenade
1/2 cup grated cheese
1 cup whole green olives
1 cup flour
1 tblsp baking powder
1/4 tsp salt

MAKE egg up to one cup with water, add tapenade, then stir in remaining ingredients until just combined. Three-quarters fill well-greased muffin pans and bake at 200°C for 12–15 minutes.

Three-Grain Pear Muffins

2 pears
1 large egg, beaten
1 cup buttermilk
2 tblsp oil
1 1/4 cups wholemeal flour
3/4 cup cornmeal
1/2 cup rolled oats
1/4 cup chopped raisins or currants
1 1/2 tsp baking powder
1/2 tsp baking soda
1 tsp cinnamon

QUARTER and core the pears, but do not peel. Grate the pears. Beat together egg, buttermilk and oil. Add pears. In separate bowl, combine remaining ingredients. Add wet ingredients to dry ingredients, and stir until just blended. Spoon into prepared muffin pans. Bake in a preheated 180°C oven for about 20–25 minutes.

Toasted Pine Nut Muffins

1 egg
1/4 cup water
1 cup natural yoghurt
50g butter, melted
2 tblsp honey
2 cups flour
1 tblsp baking powder
90g ground almonds
1/3 cup sugar
3/4 cup pine nuts, pan-fried until light brown
honey for pouring

MIX all ingredients together until just combined. Spoon into well-greased muffin pans and bake at 190°C for 15–20 minutes. Pour a little warmed honey over each muffin while still hot.

Toffee Muffins

¹/₂ cup sugar
¹/₂ cup water
¹/₃ cup oil
³/₄ cup sugar
1 egg
³/₄ cup milk
1 ³/₄ cups flour
1 ¹/₂ tsp baking powder

G ENTLY boil first measure of sugar with water until mixture turns golden brown. Pour onto greased tinfoil and leave to set. Break toffee into small pieces. Reserve some larger pieces for decorating cooked muffins. Whisk oil, second measure of sugar, egg and milk together. Add toffee and remaining ingredients, and mix until just combined. Spoon into well-greased muffin pans and bake at 190°C for 20 minutes.

Toffee Maple Muffins

$1/2$ cup sugar
$1/2$ cup water
$1/3$ cup oil
$1/2$ cup maple syrup
$1/3$ cup sugar
1 egg
$1/4$ cup milk
1 $3/4$ cups flour
1 $1/2$ tsp baking powder

BOIL first measure of sugar and water gently in pot until mixture turns golden brown. Pour onto greased tinfoil and leave to set. Break toffee into small pieces. Whisk oil, maple syrup, second measure of sugar, egg and milk together. Add toffee and remaining ingredients, mixing until just combined. Spoon into well-greased muffin pans and bake at 190°C for 20 minutes.

Toffee Walnut Muffins

$^1/_2$ cup sugar
$^1/_2$ cup water
$^1/_3$ cup oil
$^3/_4$ cup sugar
1 egg
$^3/_4$ cup milk
2 $^1/_4$ cups flour
1 $^1/_2$ tsp baking powder
1 cup walnut pieces
12 walnut halves for decoration

B OIL first measure of sugar and water gently until mixture turns golden brown. Pour onto greased tinfoil. When set, break toffee into small pieces. Whisk oil, second measure of sugar, egg and milk together. Add toffee and remaining ingredients, mixing until just combined. Three-quarters fill well-greased muffin pans and put a walnut half on top of each. Bake at 190°C for 20 minutes.

Tomato, Cheese & Oregano Muffins

1 egg
³/₄ cup water
1 ¹/₂ cups self-raising flour
1 cup grated tasty cheddar cheese
¹/₄ cup grated Parmesan cheese
1 tblsp fresh oregano (or 1 tsp dried)
3 tomatoes, seeded and chopped

M IX all ingredients together until just combined. Spoon into well-greased muffin pans and bake at 190°C for 15 minutes.

Upside-Down Rhubarb Muffins

¹/₄ cup melted butter
1 cup finely chopped rhubarb
¹/₂ cup brown sugar
¹/₃ cup soft butter
¹/₃ cup sugar
1 egg
1 ¹/₂ cups flour
2 tsp baking powder
¹/₂ tsp salt
¹/₂ tsp nutmeg
¹/₂ cup milk

COMBINE melted butter, rhubarb and brown sugar in small bowl and mix well. Spread evenly in greased muffin pans. Beat together butter, sugar and egg until fluffy. Combine flour, baking powder, salt and nutmeg and add to creamed mixture alternately with milk. Stir to just moisten, then spoon on top of rhubarb mixture. Bake at 190°C for 20–25 minutes. Invert on cooling rack and leave pan over muffins for a few minutes so all the rhubarb runs out. Serve warm.

Vanilla & Coconut Muffins

1 cup flour
1 cup coconut
1 ³/₄ tsp baking powder
3 tblsp brown sugar
2 tblsp butter, melted and cooled slightly
¹/₂ cup milk
1 egg
¹/₂ tsp vanilla essence
coconut for sprinkling
Icing
2 cups icing sugar, 1 tsp vanilla essence, 1 tblsp butter, milk to mix

IN large bowl mix together flour, coconut, baking powder and brown sugar. In separate bowl mix together butter, milk, egg and vanilla. Make well in centre of dry ingredients and add milk mixture. Stir to just combine. Spoon batter into prepared muffin pans and bake at 190°C for 10–15 minutes. Top with vanilla icing and sprinkle with coconut. To make icing, mix ingredients together.

Vanilla Poppy Seed Muffins

150g butter
$^3/_4$ cup sugar
1 egg, beaten
150g vanilla yoghurt
1 tsp vanilla essence
1 $^1/_2$ cups flour
1 tsp baking powder
1 tsp baking soda
3 tblsp poppy seeds

CREAM butter and sugar, then stir in remaining ingredients until just combined. Spoon into muffin pans lined with paper cases and bake at 160°C for 15–20 minutes.

Vegetable Muffins

5 cups flour
1 1/2 cups mixed vegetables
1/2 cup finely chopped bacon or ham
2 cups grated cheese
50g butter, melted
5 tsp baking powder
salt
1 onion or chives, finely chopped
3 eggs, beaten
1 tsp green herb stock powder
milk to mix

MIX all ingredients together with milk to make a soft dough. Spoon into greased muffin pans. Bake at 200°C for about 20 minutes. Quantities can be halved.

Wasabi Muffins

2 tblsp vegetable oil
2 tsp hot wasabi paste
3 tblsp celery, finely chopped
3 tblsp red or green pepper, finely chopped and seeds removed
1 medium onion, finely chopped
1 cup tasty or mozzarella cheese, grated
2 $^1/_2$ cups plain flour
2 tsp baking powder
$^1/_4$ tsp salt
1 egg, beaten
50g butter, melted
$^1/_2$ to 1 cup milk

B RAISE wasabi paste, celery, pepper and onion in 2 tablespoons oil until soft or brown. Add to cheese and sifted dry ingredients. Stir to combine. Add beaten egg, butter and milk to moisten. Spoon into greased muffin pans. Sprinkle a little cheese on top. Place into hot oven and bake at 200°C for 15 minutes or until golden brown.

Whiskey Raisin Muffins

1 cup raisins
1/4 cup whiskey
2 tblsp honey
1 cup yoghurt
1/4 cup milk
50g butter, melted
1 egg
2 cups flour
2 tsp baking powder
1/3 cup sugar

GENTLY heat raisins and whiskey, then leave to soak for at least an hour. Add remaining ingredients to raisins and mix until just combined. Spoon into well-greased muffin pans and bake at 180°C for 15–20 minutes.

Wholemeal Muffins

1 cup milk
1 egg, lightly beaten
2 cups wholemeal self-raising flour
$^1/_4$ cup raw sugar
$^1/_2$ cup sultanas
100g butter, melted

MIX milk and lightly beaten egg. Add all other ingredients. Mix until just combined. Three-quarters fill greased muffin pans and bake at 190°C for 15–20 minutes.

Wholemeal Spicy Pumpkin Muffins

¹/₂ cup packed brown sugar
¹/₄ cup vegetable oil
1 egg
¹/₂ cup mashed cooked pumpkin
¹/₂ cup sultanas
1 ¹/₂ cups wholemeal self-raising flour
¹/₂ tsp salt
¹/₄ tsp nutmeg
¹/₄ tsp mixed spice
¹/₂ cup milk (approx.)

BEAT together sugar, oil, egg and mashed pumpkin until well blended. Stir in sultanas. Sift flour, salt and spices. Stir into pumpkin mixture alternately with milk until just combined. Three-quarters fill greased muffin pans and bake at 200°C for 15–20 minutes.

Yoghurt & Sultana Muffins

1 cup plain flour
$^{1}/_{2}$ tsp baking powder
$^{1}/_{2}$ tsp salt
$^{1}/_{4}$ tsp baking soda
$^{3}/_{4}$ cup wheatgerm
4 tblsp packed brown sugar
1 egg, beaten
1 cup yoghurt
75g melted butter, cooled
$^{1}/_{2}$ cup sultanas
1 tblsp milk (optional)

SIFT flour, baking powder, salt and baking soda. Stir in wheatgerm and brown sugar. Combine beaten egg, yoghurt (adding milk if very thick) and cooled butter, and add to dry ingredients. Add sultanas and stir until just moistened. Do not overmix. Three-quarters fill greased muffin pans and bake at 190°C for 20–25 minutes.

Zucchini Muffins

1 egg
$1/4$ cup sugar
2 tblsp oil
$1/2$ cup buttermilk
1 $1/4$ cups wholemeal flour
1 tsp baking powder
$1/2$ tsp baking soda
2–3 tsp ground cinnamon
2 cups grated zucchini

BEAT together egg, sugar, oil and buttermilk. Combine dry ingredients. Add zucchini and wet ingredients to dry ingredients. Mix until all ingredients are just combined, and spoon into prepared muffin pans. Bake in a preheated oven at 180°C for 20–30 minutes.

Zucchini Nut Muffins

3 cups flour
1 tsp baking powder
1 tsp baking soda
$^1/_2$ tsp salt
1 tsp cinnamon
2 cups sugar
4 eggs, room temperature
1 cup canola oil
2 cups grated zucchini
$^1/_2$ tsp vanilla essence
1 cup chopped walnuts
$^1/_2$ cup raisins

PREHEAT oven to 180°C. Grease muffin pans. Sift dry ingredients (except sugar) and set aside. Combine sugar and eggs. Beat 2 minutes. Add oil and beat for 3 minutes. Add zucchini, vanilla, nuts and raisins. Fold in dry ingredients until mixed. Fill muffin pans two-thirds full and bake for 25 minutes. Wonderful with berry jam.

Zucchini Pineapple Muffins

3 eggs
2 cups sugar
1 cup oil
2 tsp vanilla essence
2 cups zucchini, grated
3 cups flour
1 tsp baking powder
1 tsp baking soda
1 tsp salt
1 cup pineapple, crushed
$^1/_2$ cup nuts, chopped (optional)
$^1/_2$ cup maraschino cherries (optional)

BEAT eggs, sugar, oil, and vanilla. Add zucchini, flour, baking powder, baking soda, salt, pineapple, nuts and cherries. Pour into prepared muffin pans. Bake at 175°C for about 20 minutes.

Zucchini & Wheatgerm Muffins

2 cups flour
¹/₂ cup wheatgerm
3 tsp baking powder
pinch salt
¹/₂ cup brown sugar
1 cup zucchini, grated
1 egg
¹/₄ cup oil
³/₄ cup milk

MIX flour, wheatgerm, baking powder and salt in bowl. Stir in sugar and zucchini. Beat egg, oil and milk together and stir into mixture until just combined. Three-quarters fill greased muffin pans and bake at 190°C for 20–25 minutes.

Index